S0-ARL-021

God Can Do Anything But Fail, So Try Parasailing In A Wind Storm

Stan Toler

Copyright © 2012, 2017 Stan Toler
God Can Do Anything Buy Fail, So Try Parasailing In A Wind Storm/Stan Toler

ISBN: 978-1-943140-06-0

Dust Jacket Press
PO Box 721243
Oklahoma City, OK 73172
www.dustjacket.com
800-495-0192

Cover Design: D.E. West, ZAQ Designs/Dust Jacket Creative Services
Interior Design: Lyn Rayn

Printed in the United States of America. All rights reserved under International Copyright Law. Contents and/or cover may not be reproduced in whole or in part in any form without th eexpress written consent of the Publisher.

Unless otherwise indicated, all Scripture quotations are from the Holy Bible, New International Version® (NIV®), Copyright © 1973, 1978, 1984 International Bible Society. Used by permission of Zondervan. All rights reserved.

Scripture taken from The Message. The Message (MSG), Copyright © 1993, 1994, 1995, 1996, 2000, 2001, 2002 by Eugene H. Peterson.

Special Thanks To: Adam Toler, Jerry Brecheisen, Deloris Leonard, Pat Diamond and Cathy Buchanan for their encouragement, editing and assistance with this project.

Contents

Introduction

**Developing A God Can
Do Anything But Fail Mindset**

*The greatest need of the church today
is for a greater number of Christians
who are not shallow or sinful,
but deep and committed.*

—John Stott

It was a lovely day in Destin, Florida. The sky was blue to perfection. The ocean was brimming with mountainous waves. As I sat on a park bench with my toes in the white sand, nearby, I saw people parasailing. As I observed the beauty of God's creation, I was seeing new courage and faith as I was reminded that my God Can Do Anything but Fail!

I was converted as a young boy in Sunday school class— just four years old. I was called to preach at age seven during a three and a half week revival under the ministry of O.W. Willis. I preached my first sermon at age fourteen and pastored my first church at age seventeen. (God bless those people in Newark, Ohio!) Recently I did an audit of my personal beliefs, while preparing to write *ReThink Your Life*, and realized that nothing significant has changed since those early days of coming to know the Lord. I still believe my God can do anything, and that shapes my entire worldview.

What do you believe? What does your faith come down to when you cut away all the philosophy and politics and theology? What it all comes down to—that simple faith in Jesus—is a powerful force in your life. Hold on to this gift as you would a costly treasure; don't let anyone steal it or devalue it. As Paul said:

Just as you received Christ Jesus as Lord, continue to live in him, rooted and built up in him, strengthened in the faith as you were taught, and overflowing with thankfulness. See to it that no one takes you captive through hollow and deceptive philosophy, which depends on human tradition and the basic principles of this world rather than on Christ.

—Col. 2:6-8

The Marks of Simple Faith

The simplicity of the gospel doesn't make it easy. It is good, beautiful, basic, and true—but not easy. Living out the faith is a bit like the old board game Othello: it takes a minute to learn, and a lifetime to master. We may accept the truth on an intellectual level but balk when we have to apply it to our lives; or we may understand in a heartbeat that Jesus loves us, but grasping the depth of what that means seems out of reach.

One of the marks of simple faith, for example, is accepting hardship gracefully. We may recite verses like James 1:3-4 ("Because you know that the testing of your faith develops perseverance. Perseverance must finish its work so that you may be mature and complete, not lacking anything."), believing the message is true—but still turn in anger from God when true hardships come our way.

If we are perfectly honest, trials are hard to accept even when they are relatively minor.

Consider the story of a teacher who was helping a kindergarten student put on his cowboy boots. Even with her pulling and him pushing, the little boots didn't want to go on. By the time they got the second boot on, she had worked up a sweat. She almost cried when the little boy said, "Teacher, they're on the wrong feet." She looked, and sure enough, they were.

It wasn't any easier pulling the boots off than it was putting them on. She managed to keep her cool as together they worked to get the boots back on, this time on the right feet. He then announced, "These aren't my boots." She bit her tongue rather than get right in his face to scream, "Why didn't you say so?"

Once again, she struggled to help him pull off the boots. No sooner had they gotten the boots off when he said, "They're my brother's boots. My mom made me wear 'em." Now she didn't know if she should laugh or cry, but she mustered up what grace and courage she had left to wrestle the boots on his feet again.

Helping him into his coat, she asked, "Now, where are your mittens?" He said, "I stuffed 'em in the toes of my boots."[1]

As hard as it may be, one of the marks of simple faith is accepting trials—large and small—with grace. Scripture takes it even further: "We also *rejoice* in our sufferings, because we know that suffering produces perseverance; character; and character, hope" (Romans 5:3–4, italics mine). When we have confidence in God's goodness and power, we can trust that He will make something good from our circumstances.

No one said simple faith makes life easy.

---

[1]John Beukema, Chambersburg, Pennsylvania.

Confidence in God

Lots of people believe in God. Many even pray to God, earnestly, especially when they find themselves in tight situations. We have to be careful, though, to determine within ourselves whether our belief in God is really faith. It's true that our faith comes down to knowing in our hearts that God is real—and I'd go so far as to say such a belief is one of the main ingredients of simple faith-but maybe "believing in God" needs to be defined.

Is it enough to believe some Santa-like being exists out there somewhere to give us things that make us happy? Is it enough to have some feeling in our gut that there has to be something bigger than ourselves, and we might as well call that something "God"? Is it even enough to have a certain knowledge that the true God of the Bible exists?

Or is simple faith something more?

Billy Graham, that great evangelist, provides us a profound example of what believing in God means. Knowing he is entering the final chapters of his life here on earth, he says, "I think about heaven a great deal. I think about the failures in my life in the past but know they have been covered by the blood of Christ. And that gives me a great sense of confidence. I have a certainty about eternity that is a wonderful thing, and I thank God for giving me that certainty. I do not fear death. I may fear a little bit about the process, but not death itself, because I think the moment that my spirit leaves this body, I will be in the presence of the Lord."

Billy Graham doesn't just believe in God; he has confidence in the Almighty.

Where does that confidence come from? It comes from knowing God deeply and intimately. Graham says, "[My wife Ruth and I] pray together and read the Bible together every night. It's a wonderful period of life for both of us."[2]

What joy we find in our hearts when we know God so well—when we have experienced his transforming love and entered into a meaningful relationship with him—that we can say confidently, along with the apostle John:

> In this way, love is made complete among us so that we will have confidence on the day of judgment, because in this world we are like him. There is no fear in love. But perfect love drives out fear, because fear has to do with punishment. The one who fears is not made perfect in love. We love because he first loved us.
>
> —1 John 4:17–19

Confidence in God is childlike, really. Confidence allows us look to Him the way a little girl might look to her father when she's afraid, knowing that he will take care of her. Because we believe in Him, we don't have to be afraid.

Scripture often compares us to sheep, and I recently discovered something about shepherding that makes this analogy come alive for me. Sheep are flighty animals. When they hear a loud noise or are startled from whatever reason, they scatter in fright. It's the shep-

---

[2]Jon Meacham, "Pilgrim's Progress," Newsweek (August 14, 2006).

herd's task to calm them down; he touches each sheep with his staff and speaks calmly to them. Amazingly, the sheep settle down because they trust the shepherd. We're like that, aren't we? We are startled by the things life brings at us, and we're apt to scatter in fright. But Jesus is not afraid, and He loves us. He touches each one of us, and speaks lovingly to us. If we know Him and trust Him, we are able to settle down and rest in His care.

Believing in God is a good first step; but childlike confidence in Yahweh, the God of Abraham, Isaac, and Jacob, is a true mark of simple faith.

Obedience to God's Will

"Jesus loves me, this I know." How many times have you sung those words in your lifetime? The lyrics to that simple tune make sense to a child. Even adults may find their eyes filling with tears as they sing along, realizing they are loved deeply and purely—and that this love comes from Jesus himself.

What do you do with that kind of love?

You respond.

Once you accept His love for what it is—a gift of grace—you can't help but *want* to show Him the depth of your appreciation; you *want* to do what will please Him. A mark of simple faith is obedience, because obedience is a response to the message of that children's song.

1 John 5:1–3 says,

Everyone who believes that Jesus is the Christ is born of God, and everyone who loves the father loves his child as well. This is how we know that we love the children of God: by loving God and carrying out his commands. This is love for God: to obey his commands. And his commands are not burdensome.

The more we fall in love with Him the more God's commands quit sounding like orders and begin sounding like good and helpful principles that enrich our lives.

Not that it's always that easy to obey God. (Are you seeing a theme here?) Obedience is not a one-time decision; it requires daily surrender to God's will. Every single day—maybe every single minute—we have to resist temptation. Even when we believe with all our hearts that Jesus loves us, we feel the pull of sin. We may understand that God's way is so much better than our way, but our way seems easier.

The apostle Paul said to believers in the early church, "Do not lie to each other, since you have taken off your old self with its practices" (Colossians 3:9). Apparently we have to be intentional about responding to God's love with obedience. We experience God's love, we trust that his way is better than ours, and we "take off" our old self. I sometimes imagine that to be like a snake shedding its skin—not exactly painful, but still a big deal.

Molting occurs periodically throughout a snake's life. Before a molt, the snake stops eating and often hides or moves to a safe place. Just before shedding, the skin becomes dull and dry looking and the eyes become cloudy or blue-colored. The inner surface of the old skin liquefies. This causes the old skin to separate from the new skin beneath it. After a few days, the eyes clear and the snake "crawls" out of its old skin. The old skin breaks near the mouth and the snake wriggles out, aided by rubbing against rough surfaces. In many cases, the cast skin peels backward over the body from head to tail in one piece, like pulling a sock off inside-out. A new, larger, brighter layer of skin has formed underneath.[3]

Wouldn't it be nice if God would snap His fingers and remove our sinful nature so we don't need to go through such a process, often more than once? Why is so hard to obey Him even when we've seen over and over again how much better it is with our "larger, brighter layer" that is revealed when we peel off our old self?

The question is a bit ironic, because our frustration with God about our imperfections reveals our lack of trust in Him. Listen to Romans 9:20–21:

> But who are you, O man, to talk back to God? Shall what is formed say to him who formed it, "Why did you make me like this?" Does not the potter have the right to make out of the same lump of clay some pottery for noble purposes and some for common use?

We may not understand why we have to keep shedding our old self in order to remain obedient before God, but I

[3]Wikipedia, October 17, 2010 http://en.wikipedia.org/wiki/Snake.

suspect He knows what He's doing. And surrendering to Him is always a good experience.

It's kind of like calling customer service. We never want to read the manual when assembling a new item. We don't want to pick up the phone when something goes wrong with a product we are using. We just want to fix the problem ourselves—or wait until it goes away. I remember a time I tried fixing a problem myself. Working for hours to get a computer program to work. I felt like I was right on the verge of figuring it out. But, I wanted the satisfaction of not needing to rely on someone else for a technical issue. Only after exhausting every idea I could possibly concoct did I finally give in and call customer service, feeling stupid for failing to figure out what should be a simple process. It was a simple process; it took them just a moment to identify the problem and to provide me with an essential file that was missing.

There are some things in life we just can't figure out on our own. We need our Creator. We'll never be able to accomplish in our entire lives what He can do for us in an instant. Surrendering to Him can come after a long battle of failures, or we can happily let God lead us the right way from the beginning.

A mark of simple faith is obedience—and the results are always better than we think.

Growth in Grace

Have you ever planted a garden? It's exciting to place those seeds in the carefully tilled ground, anticipating the flowers or vegetables that will eventually sprout. Of course, planting the seeds is only the first step in gardening; the hard part comes next: weeding. The interesting thing is that if you skip this step, growth will still happen—it's just that the wrong thing will grow. Your plants will likely be choked by the more aggressive weeds.

Likewise, a person does not remain unchanged. Each of us either grow fruits of the Spirit, or we allow weeds to prosper in our spiritual garden. It would be a mistake to think that we can leave our spiritual lives untended without any negative results.

The world is ordered in such a way that things need to be tended. If they're not, they decline. What happens if you leave water trapped in one place? It turns stagnant. What happens if you quit maintaining your home? The paint peels and the wood rots. What happens if you don't pay attention to your relationships? You end up in a fight. What happens if you quit reading? Your mind loses its sharpness. What happens if you don't exercise and eat nutritiously? You gain weight. What happens if a football team quits practicing? They won't win their games.

You get the idea.

God didn't intend for us to remain unchanged. He wants us to grow. The good news is that He empowers us to grow. After we receive the grace of God, we are transformed. The apostle Paul says, "Therefore, there is now no condemnation for those who are in Christ Jesus" (Romans 8:1). What an exciting gospel! We don't have to continue plodding in our sin; we are free! We don't have to live the old way anymore; we can embrace the new life Christ offers us, and grow in grace.

Jeremiah 17:6 encourages us to tend our spiritual garden. "Just as you received Christ Jesus as Lord [seeds planted], continue to live in him [weeds tended]." Walk with Jesus, moving forward don't allow yourself to become stagnant.

Spiritual maturity and wisdom are not an aspiration only for an elite group of people-the "great" Christian leaders among us. *Each* of us have been called to walk hand-in-hand with our Lord. He can tend us and grow us into something beautiful. Growing in grace is a mark of simple faith; it reveals that we are humbly walking with Jesus.

To grow, of course, we have to have strong roots. As we stretch ourselves heavenward, we have to be digging deep so we can maintain our balance. Scripture says about the godly person:

He will be like a tree planted by the water that sends out its roots by the stream. It does not fear when heat comes; its leaves are always green. It has no worries in a year of drought and never fails to bear fruit.

—Jeremiah 17:8

Being rooted is an agricultural term. My friend, David Graves frequently says, "Just as a great tree is deeply rooted in the soil and draws nourishment from it, so the Christian is rooted in Christ, the Source of life and strength."

But, it is more than that. We are built up, which is an architectural phrase. Graves says, "Just as a house stands strong because it is built on a strong foundation, so the

Christian life is resistant to any storm because it is founded on the strength of Christ."

When we are walking with Jesus, we are grounded and unleashed, rooted and built up, firm and flexible. It's a wonderful paradox—one that only those with simple faith can understand.

Love for God's Family

You may have heard the tongue-in-cheek expression, "I love the church; it's people I can't stand." We laugh but probably because we know how true that statement can feel at times. Loving each other is hard work. And it's no wonder: Causing division among Christians is our enemy's strategy. The only way to resist Satan's traps is by the power of Christ.

> For everyone born of God overcomes the world. This is the victory that has overcome the world, even our faith. Who is it that overcomes the world? Only he who believes that Jesus is the Son of God. This is the one who came by water and blood— Jesus Christ. He did not come by water only, but by water and blood. And it is the Spirit who testifies, because the Spirit is the truth. For there are three that testify: the Spirit, the water and the blood; and the three are in agreement.
>
> —1 John 5:4–8

Jesus won a battle against the enemy through great sacrifice on His part, a battle that we simply could not compete in. It's only by having faith in Christ that we can overcome the Prince of this world. It's by depending entirely on our Savior that we can live in unity and love with each other.

If we base our love for each other on good feelings or best intentions, we'll eventually fail. Loving each other through disagreements and hurt feelings and mistakes—which will inevitably arise in a church—requires us to have the love of Christ in us. And that love is available to us only when we are baptized in Him—in other words, when we die to self and are raised up in him.

Of course, the ritual itself is nothing magical. A person could be baptized without ever dying to self. Likewise, a person could fake Christlike love, at least for a while. It doesn't work long term, though. Richard Foster says, "Superficiality is the curse of our day." When we are nice to each other without really loving each other, when we are pleasant and agreeable while murmuring insults under our breath, we are creating danger—like a layer of thin ice that appears firm. Instead, in faith, we must rely on Christ to transform our hearts so our love is genuine, deep, and not easily broken.

Loving the family of God is a mark of simple faith because it reveals Christ in us.

1

God Can Love Me Even When I Don't Write On His Facebook Wall

A new command I give you: Love one another.
As I have loved you, so you must love one another.
By this all men will know that you are my
disciples, if you love one another.

—John 13:34–35

A young couple, very much in love, was getting married in church. However, Sue, the young bride, confided in the pastor that she was nervous about the big occasion; so the minister chose one verse that he felt would be a great encouragement to them—1 John 4:18, which says, "There is no fear in love, but perfect love casts out fear."

A few days before the wedding, the pastor asked the best man to read the verse out loud during the wedding ceremony. The best man gladly accepted the invitation, proud to have such an important role. He was not a regular churchgoer and not very familiar with the Bible so he looked the verse up ahead of time to practice. The verse seemed a bit strange to him, but he figured the pastor knew what he was talking about. Still, he called the pastor just to be sure it was the right verse.

"Yes, yes," the pastor said. "I had a private talk with Sue this morning, and I know this verse is perfect for her. In fact, you might say that before you read it. I think it will mean a lot to her."

The big day came. The best man waited for his cue, and then opened up the Bible to the bookmarked page, saying, "Sue, the pastor felt this verse was tailor made for you." He proceeded to read, in clear voice, for all the church to hear, the verse from the book of John—instead of the first letter of John! He read: "You have five husbands and the one that you now have is not your husband."

We may mix up scripture passages, but we'll never mix up the fact that God is love. Love is basic and essential to our faith. The greatest discovery of the human heart is the love of God. God loves us—we know this, we live this, we breathe this. And He loves us in so many ways.

God's Love Is Extravagant

Unmerited

In the book, "Children's Letters to God: The New Collection," a little girl named Nan writes this letter: "Dear God, I bet it is very hard for you to love all of everybody in the whole world. There are only four people in our family and I have trouble loving them!"

Thankfully, God does love everybody in the whole world, even though we're not exactly the easiest people to live with. We reject Him, disobey Him and neglect Him. We are ashamed of Him, we use His name to defend our unholy cause, and we ignore His people. And before we did these awful things, God knew we would and yet He loves us.

> God put his love on the line for us by offering his Son in sacrificial death while we were of no use whatever to him.
>
> —Romans 5:8, THE MESSAGE

Forgiving

Heather Gemmen Wilson was raped at knifepoint in her own home by a stranger while her husband was at a church meeting and her young children slept in the next room. Heather lived to tell the story, but the nightmare continued: she found out she was pregnant as a result of the rape. Now Heather shares her story publicly, proud to show off the beautiful daughter she believes God handpicked for her. "The key to healing is forgiveness," Heather says, "but forgiveness isn't minimizing what happened. It's recognizing how ugly and awful it was—and letting go anyway."

God's eyes are wide open when He looks at our sin. He knows exactly how we have let Him down. And God cannot abide such behavior. He won't just brush it aside as if what we did was no big deal, thereby degrading Himself; but He won't turn away from us either. He loves us, and wants to gather us to Himself. That's why He sent His Son to cleanse us from our sin and to make us right with Him.

This is how God showed his love for us: God sent his only Son into the world so we might live through him. This is the kind of love we are talking about—not that we once upon a time loved God, but that he loved us and sent his Son as a sacrifice to clear away our sins and the damage they've done to our relationship with God.

—1 John 4:9–11, THE MESSAGE

Free

During a British conference on comparative religions, experts from around the world debated what, if any, belief was unique to the Christian faith. They began eliminating possibilities. Incarnation? Other religions had different versions of gods appearing in human form. Resurrection? Again, other religions had accounts of return from death.

The debate went on for some time until C. S. Lewis wandered into the room. "What's the rumpus about?" he asked, and heard in reply that his colleagues were discussing Christianity's unique contribution among world religions. Lewis responded, "Oh, that's easy. It's grace." After some discussion, the conferees had to agree.

The notion of God's love coming to us free of charge, no strings attached, seems to go against every instinct of humanity. The Buddhist eightfold path, the Hindu doctrine of Karma, the Jewish covenant, and the Muslim code of law—each offers a way to earn approval. Only Christianity dares to make God's love unconditional.[4]

Watch what God does, and then you do it, like children who learn proper behavior from their parents. Mostly what God does is love you. Keep company with him and learn a life of love. Observe how Christ loved us. His love was not cautious but extravagant. He didn't love in order to get something from us but to give everything of himself to us. Love like that.
—Ephesians 5:12 THE MESSAGE

[4]Philip Yancey, *What's So Amazing about Grace?* (Zondervan, 1997).

God's Love Is Intimate

Personal

A village once had a huge statue that everyone honored; the problem was it was so immense that you couldn't see exactly what it represented. Someone finally miniaturized the statue so everyone could see the person it honored.

"That is what God did in his Son," said the early church father Origen. Paul tells us Christ is the visible icon or image of the invisible God (Colossians 1). In Christ we have God in a comprehensible way. In Christ, we have God's own personal and definitive visit to the planet.[5]

God can be known, and He knows you personally. He doesn't sell a one-size-fits-all kind of love; He sees you specifically, and gives you exactly what you need. Max Lucado writes, "God's list contains the name of every person who ever lived. For this is the scope of his love. And this is the reason for the cross. He loves the world."[6]

Are not two sparrows sold for a penny? Yet not one of them will fall to the ground apart from the will of your Father. And even the very hairs of your head are all numbered. So don't be afraid; you are worth more than many sparrows.

—Matthew 10:29–31

---

[5]Dale Bruner, "Is Jesus Inclusive or Exclusive?" Theology, News & Notes (October 1999).
[6]"He Chose the Nails."

Embracing

Recently, I read an article about Elizabeth Smart. You may recall that she was kidnapped and held hostage for several months. She's now a well-adjusted person. There were moments, she said, when she felt despair, "but I always knew that no matter what I'd still be a part of my family. They could change my name, change the way I look, but they couldn't change the fact that I am Ed and Lois Smart's daughter. That was powerful to me."

When you know whom you belong to, that secret in your heart carries you for a long time. Likewise, God knows that you belong to Him, and He will never forget. You are his precious child.

> How great is the love the Father has lavished on us, that we should be called children of God! And that is what we are! The reason the world does not know us is that it did not know him.
>
> —1 John 3:1

Inviting

He was just a shoemaker, and an average one at that. However, in the evenings, after work, he studied Greek, Hebrew, and a variety of modern languages. He devoured Captain Cook's *Voyages* to expand his horizons, which, because of his poverty, kept him bound to a small, forgotten English village. Some people said his time would have been better spent getting a second job to support his growing family.

But the young man's passion wasn't a curious, self-satisfying hobby. Early in life he had become concerned about the millions of unbelievers outside of Europe, and he was trying to figure out what could be done to bring them the gospel. With God's help, he slowly figured it out. He ended up going to India to serve as the first Protestant missionary in the modern era. His passion inspired a generation of men and women, such as Adoniram Judson, Hudson Taylor, and David Livingstone, to take up the cause of missions.

Because one impoverished shoemaker named William Carey followed his God-given passion, large parts of the world that had little or no access to the gospel have large populations of people today who confess Christ as Lord.[7]

God calls us into His service—not because we're so notable or because He can't do it himself. He calls us so we have the opportunity to make a difference in His Kingdom.

> As Jesus went on from there, he saw a man named Matthew sitting at the tax collector's booth. "Follow me," he told him, and Matthew got up and followed him.
>
> —Matthew 9:9

---

[7]Ruth Tucker, From Jerusalem to Irian Jaya (Zondervan, 1983).

God's Love Is Universal

Reaching

I spent time with an old friend, Melvin Hatley, recently. He reminded me of how his family came to Christ and the Church of the Nazarene. The evangelist Holland London and Rev. Jimmy Dobson stopped and visited with Melvin and his family on the front porch of their humble home and invited them to church. Melvin's mother said, "We have no clothes and our boys have no shoes." Sister Dobson, who is the mother of James Dobson and was a pastor's wife in Sulphur Springs, Texas, went out and got them clothes. The family went to church and that day accepted Christ. Today, Melvin is part of a great family of faith, leaders in the church.

God has placed us in community so that we can support each other, draw each other to Him, and love each other. We're not meant to just sit in our own little bubble; we're meant to reach out to others.

> For God so loved the world that he gave his one and only Son, that whoever believes in him shall not perish but have eternal life.
>
> —John 3:16

Including

I believe many people drive by our churches and think about it as a golfer would think about a country club: "I'd like to play the course, but I'm not a member." If you

God Can Do Anything But Fail

were not a member at your church, would you be welcome there? If you didn't know the rules or the expectations, and you showed up looking odd and doing all the wrong things, would people receive you warmly?

Story after story in the Gospels reveals how Jesus loved. He didn't form a club with a secret handshake that only elite people could join. He loved everyone. He loved His close friends and strangers; he loved those who were good to Him and those who were unlovable.

> Brothers, think of what you were when you were called. Not many of you were wise by human standards; not many were influential; not many were of noble birth. But God chose the foolish things of the world to shame the wise; God chose the weak things of the world to shame the strong. He chose the lowly things of this world and the despised things—and the things that are not—to nullify the things that are.
>
> —1 Corinthians 1:26–28

Unconditional

A minister was speaking about all the things money can't buy. "Money can't buy happiness; it can't buy laughter, and money can't buy love," he told the congregation. Driving his point home, he said, "What would you do if I offered you $1,000 not to love your mother and father?" A hush fell over the congregation. Finally, a small voice near the front raised an important question, "How much would you give me not to love my sister?"

God is not going to quit loving you for all the money in the world, and you don't have to pay Him a cent to make Him love you. Even better than that, God loves you whether or not you love Him back—and will pursue you gently and patiently all your days.

> And this is the testimony: God has given us eternal life, and this life is in his Son.
>
> —1 John 5:11-12

God's Love Is Sufficient

Timely

A retired United Methodist pastor and his wife left their home before hurricane Katrina struck and went to a shelter. After the storm passed, Rev. Jones and his wife were allowed back into the city to grab a few belongings. When they entered their house the water was still knee-high, but Jones was determined to see what he could salvage.

He saw several framed family photos floating in the water, but nothing else worth saving. He quickly grabbed the pictures and left. Back at the shelter, he took the photos out of their frames so they could dry out. When he removed his father's picture, money fell out of the frame. He was astonished to count out $366. Even more astounding was that his father had died in 1942, when Jones himself was only twelve years old. He had no idea the money was in the frame.

The money was precisely what he and his wife needed to get to Atlanta after the storm to live with their daughter.[8]

God isn't late with his promise as some measure lateness. He is restraining himself on account of you, holding back the End because he doesn't want anyone lost. He's giving everyone space and time to change.

—2 Peter 3:9 THE MESSAGE

Real

Werner "Jack" Genot wanted to be a hero. So, he concocted a story about serving as a marine and being taken as a prisoner of war during a bloody Korean War battle.

Genot, now seventy-one, is from the small Illinois town of Marengo, where he serves as an alderman. His story grew until the uniform he wore on special occasions became laden with fake medals he had ordered from a catalog—a Bronze Star, a Silver Star, and two Purple Hearts. He would march in parades and talk to school-children. He even got a special license plate reserved for wounded veterans by forging discharge papers.

However, a veteran's league eventually noticed a lack of records on file and numerous factual holes in Genot's military record and began an investigation. For two years, Genot denied the accusations and danced around the questions. But he finally confessed his deception in

---

[8]Told by Douglas Heiman, Evansville, Indiana.

an interview with a local newspaper, claiming he could no longer stand the facade.[9]

With stories like that, it's no wonder we question the authenticity of God and His love for us. God's record, however, is clean—established before time began and extending through eternity. Dig all you want, but you'll find no holes. God's love for us will never fail.

"God told them, 'I've never quit loving you and never will. Expect love, love, and more love!'"

—Jeremiah 31:3, THE MESSAGE

Patient

We are not a patient people. A survey of 1,003 adults done in 2006 by the Associated Press and Ipsos discovered the following:

- While waiting in line at an office or store, most people take an average of seventeen minutes to lose their patience.
- On hold on the phone most people lose their patience in nine minutes.
- Women lost their patience after waiting in line for about eighteen minutes. Men lost it after fifteen minutes.
- People with lower income and less education are more patient than those with a college education and a high income.

God Can Do Anything But Fail

34

[9]Jeff Long, "He Lied So He Could Be a Hero," Chicago Tribune (November 22, 2005).
[10]Trevor Tompson, "Impatience-Poll Glance," www.hosted.ap.org (May 28, 2006).

- People who live in the suburbs are more patient than people who live in the city.[10]

God doesn't have the same problem we have with impatience. Obviously, eighteen minutes in view of eternity is less than a drop in the bucket. He is omniscient, and having the broad scope gives Him the ability to put things in perspective. Don't worry; God's not going to throw a temper tantrum when things aren't going well; He's not going to pull out of an investment fund when the economy is bad. And He's not going to lose his patience with you.

The LORD is compassionate and gracious, slow to anger, abounding in love.
—Psalm 103:8

God's Love Is Transforming

Individualized

Deleese Williams, a woman who was promised cosmetic surgeries on *Extreme Makeover* that would "transform her life and destiny," has sued the producers of the hit TV show. That dream was shattered when one of the dental surgeons reported that Williams' recovery time would be longer than expected. She was pulled from the show the night before her surgeries were scheduled to begin and sent home to Texas.

According to the lawsuit, Williams sobbed uncontrollably when she was given the news. "How can I go back as ugly as I left?" she said, "I was supposed to come home pretty." Deleese is hurt and humiliated; more than that, her relationship with her family has been damaged, as the producers had coached family members not to accept Deleese's physical flaws and pushed them to verbally express their opinions on taped interviews-which Deleese later saw.[11]

What an extreme tragedy! Thank goodness, God's love does not tear us down, nor does He ever abandon us. It's because He sees our true beauty, as the work of His own hands, that He loves us. It's because of His great love for us that He transforms us into new creations, spotless and pure before Him—not on the outside with plastic surgery, but on the inside with chords of love.

> Being confident of this, that he who began a good work in you will carry it on to completion until the day of Christ Jesus.
>
> —Philippians 1:6

Societal

When I was in High School, a popular song was "What the World Needs Now Is Love Sweet Love" by Hal David. It was released on April 15, 1965, and reached number 7 on the US charts in May of that year. I don't think the song was so popular just because the tune was catchy; its message is just as profound today as it was back then.

---

[11]Michelle Caruso, "Extreme Tragedy," nydailynews.com (September 18, 2005).

What the world needs now is love sweet love,
It's the only thing that there's just too little of.
What the world needs now is love sweet love,
No not just for some but for everyone.

It's a rough world. We keep hoping things will improve, but as long as that hope is based on humanity finally behaving themselves, it's an empty dream. Nothing will change our world, except the love of God.

Imagine if everyone knew, profoundly and deeply, the love of God. Imagine His love manifested in each person. Don't you think violence, crime, poverty, even rudeness would cease? God is concerned with individuals, and changes their hearts; but He's also concerned with the state of the world—and commissioning us to transform it with His love.

Jesus replied, "If anyone loves me, he will obey my teaching. My Father will love him, and we will come to him and make our home with him. He who does not love me will not obey my teaching. These words you hear are not my own; they belong to the Father who sent me."

—John 14:23-24

Motivational

Try getting a teenager out of bed in the morning on a school day; it's pretty tough. Then tell her that her boyfriend is calling, and watch how she pops out of bed in a hurry. Motivation is everything.

The love of God is better than a phone call from a sweetheart to get us excited about life. Okay, so telling a teenager that God loves her may not get her to pop out of bed; but when she discovers the power of His love for herself, the experience will shape her decisions, her happiness, her relationships, and her entire life. It's true for all of us.

And I ask him that with both feet planted firmly on love, you'll be able to take in with all Christians the extravagant dimensions of Christ's love. Reach out and experience the breadth! Test its length! Plumb the depths! Rise to the heights! Live full lives, full in the fullness of God.

—Ephesians 3:17-19, THE MESSAGE

Redeeming

"The Little Girl," a ballad sung by John Michael Montgomery, tells the sad story of a little girl who hid behind the couch while her drug-addicted mother and alcoholic father continually fought. They never went to church or spoke of the Lord, except in vain. The parents eventually died in a murder-suicide. The state placed the child in a foster home where she got kisses and hugs every day. The foster parents took the little girl to Sunday school where she saw a picture of Jesus hanging on a cross. With a smile, the girl pointed to the man in the picture. "I don't know His name," the little girl said. "But I know He got off the cross, because He was there in my old house. He held me close to his side as I hid behind our couch the night that my parents died."

God Can Do Anything But Fail

God's specialty is making something beautiful out of ugliness. He loves us radically, passionately, without restraint—and He will do whatever it takes to transform the pain of our lives into an intimate connection with him. He is our Redeemer.

> O Love that will not let me go,
> I rest my weary soul in Thee.
> I give Thee back the life I owe,
> That in Thine ocean depths its flow
> May richer, fuller be.
> —George Matheson[12]

And we know that in all things God works for the good of those who love him, who have been called according to his purpose.

—Romans 8:28

[11]Sing to the Lord, O Love That Will Not Let Me Go (Kansas City, Lillenas Publishing Co., 1993) p. 474.

2

God Can Forgive Me and Forget It, Even When I Forget To Forgive It

In him we have redemption through his blood, the forgiveness of sins, in accordance with the riches of God's grace that he lavished on us with all wisdom and understanding.

—Ephesians 1:7–8

A teacher in Sunday school asked the class of Junior High boys, "Can anyone here tell me what you must do before you can be forgiven for sin?"

After a brief pause one boy spoke up, "I think you 'gotta sin."

Forgiveness is not an easy thing to comprehend. Even if we could recite the definition by heart, we wouldn't necessarily understand it. It's not a bad idea, though, to start at that basic level. What is forgiveness?

Webster's gives a noun and a verb form of the verb:

n the act of forgiving
vb 1a: to give up resentment of or claim to requital for [~ an insult];
2: to cease to feel resentment against (an offender);
PARDON

The Greek meaning of the word *aphiemi*, which is often translated in our Bibles as "forgive," is "to cancel, to send away, to release."

That's what our God does. He pardons us. He cancels our sin. He sends our sins as far away as the east is from the west. Let's explore what that means for you.

The Need for Forgiveness

A shoplifter wrote to a department store, saying, "I've just become a Christian, and I can't sleep at night because I feel guilty. So here's $100 that I owe you." He signed his name then added a little PS: "If I still can't sleep, I'll send you the rest."[13]

Whether or not we feel guilty for our sin, we need forgiveness. Whenever we do something that is wrong, we are separated from God—and forgiveness is the only thing that will bring us back into His presence. Paul says, "My conscience is clear, but that does not make me innocent. It is the Lord who judges me" (1 Corinthians 4:4).

Feeling guilty is an unpleasant feeling, and most of us try to avoid it. It does have its benefits, however. Think of guilt as a sensation of wrongdoing, just as pain is a sensation of injury. What if you couldn't feel the knife cutting into you while slicing vegetables? You might slice right through your finger! What if you never felt guilt? You might continue down your destructive path.

> My guilt has overwhelmed me like a burden too heavy to bear. My wounds fester and are loathsome because of my sinful folly.
>
> —Psalm 38:4–5

Knowing how we have hurt God and others *should* create guilt in us—and that guilt should drive us to grace.

---

[13]Bill White, Paramount, California.

Our Disobedience

John Wesley says, "Sin is the willful transgression of a known law of God." And we've all done it. Scripture says, "For all have sinned and fall short of the glory of God" (Romans 3:23). Some of us sin more often and more blatantly and more destructively than others—but we're talking pass/fail here. All sin separates us from God, and every one of us has failed. We're not graded on the curve.

We each have disobeyed, so each of us has guilt.

Rob Morgan says there are three ways we deal with guilt:

By Drowning It. Some of us feel our guilt so acutely and don't know what to do with it, that we try to drown it out by indulging in things like drugs, alcohol, promiscuity—or even with good things, like food, reading, church work. We can't make the guilt go away, so we try to distract ourselves from feeling it. Marlow Brando, an American actor, ballooned to over 400 pounds; his explanation was: "I'm a guilty old man who's ashamed of the kind of life I've led. There's nothing left for me except eating."

By Denying It. Some of us fool ourselves into thinking we don't ever do anything wrong. Nice, churchgoing folk or psychopathic killers could be equally vulnerable to this delusional belief. All it takes is the skill of justification. If we can convince ourselves that we deserve better, or that we're above the law, or that we're not as bad as others, or that we're not hurting anyone else, or that God knows how stressed we are and would understand why we did it—then we are capable of denial.

By Deflecting It. Some of us don't allow ourselves to feel the weight of guilt, but we're not willing to deny it either. If denial is shoving our guilt in the deepest corner of a closet so we won't see it, deflecting is turning it into a powerless coffee-table centerpiece. John Henry Newman illustrates this pattern with his question, "How can we understand forgiveness if we haven't recognized the depth of our sin?" Guilt becomes so much more tolerable when we study it from interesting angles rather than feel its potency.

Our Accountability

Nancy Ortberg tells about her experience working in an emergency room. One of her patients was a two-year-old boy named Billy who seemed to have a bad case of asthma. For about a year, his parents frequently showed up with him at the ER when he was short of breath, and Billy was often sent to ICU. The medical staff was mystified by the recurrence of his problem, and no one was satisfied that the problem really was asthma—as neither the boy nor his family had a history of it, and there weren't obvious signs of allergies that would cause it. Finally, one of the medical interns had a breakthrough with the case: he discovered a jellybean deep in Billy's nose.[14]

Just as Billy was having symptoms without anyone knowing the cause of the problem, we're going to be accountable for our actions whether we know what they are or not. We have to go deep within ourselves,

[14]Nancy Ortberg, in the sermon "Matters of the Heart," Willow Creek Church Seeds Tape Ministry, South Barrington, Illinois.

God Can Do Anything But Fail

praying to the Holy Spirit to show us our sins and weak-nesses—even when what we find isn't pretty.

Guilt is a heavy load, and the only place we can bring it is to the Cross. Scripture assures us that one day, we will be held accountable for our actions:

> For we must all appear before the judgment seat of Christ, that each one may receive what is due him for the things done while in the body, whether good or bad.
> —2 Corinthians 5:10

The day is coming when we will have to carry the burden of our sins to the foot of Jesus. The good news is that we can bring it to Him freely now and ask for mercy rather than judgment.

The Process of Forgiveness

Max Lucado makes no claim to being a good golfer, but he loves to play and watch. So when he was invited to attend the Masters Golf Tournament by pro golfer Scott Simpson, he was thrilled.

> Off we went to Augusta National Country Club in Georgia where golf heritage hangs like moss from the trees. I was a kid in a candy store. It wasn't enough to see the course and walk the grounds; I wanted to see the locker room, where the clubs of Ben Hogan and Paul Azinger are displayed.

But they wouldn't let me in. A guard stopped me at the entrance. I showed him my pass, but he shook his head. I told him I knew Scott, but that didn't matter. "Only caddies and players," he explained. Well, he knew I wasn't a player or a caddie. Caddies are required to wear white coveralls. So I left, knowing I had made it all the way to the door but was denied entrance.

God has one requirement for entrance into heaven: that we be clothed in Christ.

When someone prays, "Take away my [sinful] rags and clothe me in your grace," Jesus, in an act visible only to the eyes of heaven, removes the stained robe and replaces it with his robe of Righteousness.

Jesus put on our coat of sin and wore it to the cross. As he died, his blood flowed over our sins and they were cleansed. Because of this, we have no fear of being turned away at the door of heaven.[15]

We bring our guilt to the foot of the cross because our heavenly Father invites us to. He wants to take it from us, to replace our heavy burden with uplifting joy.

All the prophets testify about him that everyone who believes in him receives forgiveness of sins through his name.

—Acts 10:43

---

[15]Max Lucado, "Back Door," *Christian Reader* (May–June 2000).

There is no formula for forgiveness. Carefully following an instruction manual through thirty steps will not guarantee perfectly constructed grace. No literal road signs point to the path to the cross. Scripture does, however, enlighten us with the way to salvation.

Begins with a Crisis

An atheist was walking through the woods, admiring all the "accidents" that evolution had created. "What majestic trees! What powerful rivers! What beautiful animals!" he said. Suddenly he heard a rustling in the bushes behind him. Turning to look, he saw a seven-foot grizzly bear charging toward him. He ran as fast as he could up the path.

He looked over his shoulder and saw the grizzly was closing in on him. He was so scared that tears came to his eyes. His heart was pounding. He tried to run faster but then tripped and fell to the ground. He rolled over to pick himself up, but the bear was over him, raising its right paw to strike him.

"O my God!" cried the atheist.

Time stopped. The bear froze. The forest was silent. Even the river stopped moving.

As a bright light shone on the man, a voice came out of the sky, "You deny my existence for all these years, teach others that I don't exist, and even credit creation to a cosmic accident. Do you expect me to help you out of this predicament? Am I to count you as a believer?"

The atheist looked directly into the light and said, "I would feel like a hypocrite to become a Christian after all these years, but perhaps you could make the bear a Christian?"

"Very well," said the voice.

The light went out. The river ran. The sounds of the forest resumed. Then the bear dropped its right paw, brought both paws together, bowed its head, and spoke: "Lord, for this food which I am about to receive, I am truly thankful."

What kind of crisis would it take for you to realize how much you need the Lord?

> Endure hardship as discipline; God is treating you as sons. For what son is not disciplined by his father?
> —Hebrews 12:7

Involves Full Confession

Confession, perhaps, is the main ingredient in the imprecise recipe of forgiveness.

Once we realize we need the Lord, we tell Him. We look carefully at all the sins of our life, or our day, which have created such a heavy burden of guilt, and we tell Him about it. God already know, of course, but He wants us to voice our regret so we can find true healing.

> Repent, then, and turn to God, so that your sins may be wiped out, that times of refreshing may come from the Lord.
> —Acts 3:19

It would be much more comfortable for us if God would take our burden away from us without our having to confess it, don't you think? But we would never understand the tremendous value of the gift of grace if it were that easy. As Dietrich Bonhoffer says, "Cheap grace is the preaching of forgiveness without requiring repentance."

If we confess our sins, he is faithful and just and will forgive us our sins and purify us from all unrighteousness.

—1 John 1:9

Continues with Commitment

Making Jesus our personal Savior and receiving his forgiveness is exciting beyond words. Most people remember the moment they first gave their lives to Christ because it was so significant to them. Each Christian has his or her own B.C. and A.D. calendar.

The A.D. life is all about making Jesus Lord, not just Savior. Calling Jesus your Lord means that you recognize that He is the master. It means living for him instead of for yourself. Living this way enriches your life in ways you could never imagine, but pushing aside your personal agenda does take an intentional effort—and perseverance.

Let us not become weary in doing good, for at the proper time we will reap a harvest if we do not give up.

—Galatians 6:9

Requires Complete Consecration

When Jesus is your Savior and Lord, something mystical happens: You become a new creation. Obedience to Christ becomes more than just following rules; it becomes a way of life. You may still make mistakes—even huge blunders—but you are blameless before God because you repent with true godly sorrow, fully desiring to live in a way that is pleasing to him. You are a new person.

> You were taught, with regard to your former way of life, to put off your old self, which is being corrupted by its deceitful desires; to be made new in the attitude of your minds.
>
> —Ephesians 4:22-23

The Benefits of Forgiveness

My son Adam loved playing ball for Coach Winters in Bethany, Oklahoma. I will never forget going to the game to watch the Bethany Middle School boys basketball team who were playing another area team. Both teams had warmed-up and the game had started. In short order, Coach Winters' team was down 10-2—and then something very unusual happened. The time-keeper sounded the buzzer and called the officials to the scorer's table. A mistake had occurred. You see, the teams had warmed up at one basket, but once the game started, they were shooting at wrong baskets. The embarrassed officials had not caught the mistake.

Coach Winters, a man who is up on his basketball rules, said to the official, "You know the rule, we're 10 and they're 2." The official agreed and the scorekeeper changed the score on the scoreboard. The other coach was not pleased and proceeded to argue, but the rule stood.

Play was ready to resume when Coach Winter's turned around and walked back to the referee. "Wait a minute," he said. "I know the rule, but there's another way to handle this. Why don't we just start the game over and get it right." And that's exactly what they did. They started over.

That is what we get to do when we receive forgiveness. Nothing we've done so far counts anymore. We hit the restart button.

Let's take a look at Ephesians 1:3-10 to see what some of the other benefits of salvation are. Frankly, I would be uncomfortable telling you to come to Jesus so you can be rewarded—it seems like we should come to the Almighty God out of obedience and reverence—but God himself entices us with promises of good things. He must know us well.

The Joy of Being Chosen

Praise be to the God and Father of our Lord Jesus Christ, who has blessed us in the heavenly realms with every spiritual blessing in Christ. For he chose us in him before the creation of the world to be holy and blameless in his sight.

—Romans 1:3-4

Do you remember your elementary school days when you waited with the rest of the crowd while the two team captains called kids one by one to join their teams—and you were hoping against hope that you wouldn't be the last one picked? You don't need to worry about that anymore. You have been chosen by God!

A Sense of Belonging

> In love he predestined us to be adopted as his sons through Jesus Christ, in accordance with his pleasure and will.
>
> —Romans 1:5

When M. Craig Barnes was a child, his father brought home a twelve-year-old boy named Roger, whose parents had died from a drug overdose. There was no one to care for Roger, so the Barneses decided they would raise him as their own.

> At first it was difficult for Roger to adjust to his new home. Several times a day, I heard my parents saying to Roger, "No, no. That's not how we behave in this family." "No, no. You don't have to scream or fight or hurt other people to get what you want." "No, no, Roger, we expect you to show respect in this family."
>
> In time, Roger began to change. Did he have to make those changes to become part of the family? No. He was part of the family by the grace of my

father. But did he have to work hard because he was in the family? You bet he did. It was tough for Roger to change, and he had to work at it. But he was motivated by gratitude for the amazing love he had received.[16]

We belong to the family of God when we accept Jesus Christ as our Lord and Savior. We're accepted not because we have anything to offer, but because God loves us. We move from being an outcast to being a beloved child.

Being adopted is a powerful experience, one that transforms us. Belonging to God changes us, and we live up to the status He gives us: children of God.

Grace

To the praise of his glorious grace, which he has freely given us in the One he loves.

—Romans 1:6

Archie Moore, heavy weight champion from yesterday, once got knocked down in a fight. After a tense moment, he managed to get back up—and then won the fight. Afterwards, a reporter asked him, "What were you think-ing while on the mat?" His answer: "I'm the champ! I don't belong here."

Grace is the gift that enables us to know that we are winners in the ring of life. Grace picks us up when we

[16]M. Craig Barnes, in the sermon "The Blessed Trinity," National Presbyterian Church, Washington, D.C. (May 30, 1999).

are down and puts the prize in our hands—not because we mustered up the strength from deep within, but because when we had nothing left God empowered us.

Waking up Christmas morning to discover a giant mound of presents isn't as magical as the gift of God's grace. Grace is more precious than gold, more costly than silver, more beautiful than rubies. And this invaluable gift is selected personally for you.

Redemption

> In him we have redemption through his blood.
>
> —Romans 1:7a

In the early 1500s, the artist Michelangelo spent five years painting the ceiling of the Sistine Chapel in Rome. I can't imagine what a laborious job that must have been. Keeping my arms up long enough to change a lightbulb is hard enough—and he was painting in intricate detail, hour after hour!

When the masterful art started to fade, which happened almost right away, everyone must have been disheartened, sure that no one would be able to revive the work or improve on it. They knew a masterpiece was poised over their heads, but it was inaccessible to them. Painter Biagio Biagetti said in 1936, "We see the colors of the Sistine ceiling as if through smoked glass."

In 1981, two men came up with a plan. They created a solution that they hoped would wash away the grime that covered the painting and tested a small corner of the ceiling. Incredibly, it worked! They washed the entire ceiling—taking twice as long to wash it as it had taken to paint it—and revealed the original vibrant colors and striking beauty.

That's what redemption is—being restored to our original beauty. Dignity has always been deep within us, but redemption clears away the grime that once made the dignity impossible to see.

Forgiveness

The forgiveness of sins, in accordance with the riches of God's grace.
—Romans 1:7b

You may have received forgiveness from a friend or family member, only to have that "forgiven sin" thrown back in your face sometime later. God's forgiveness is complete. His abundance of grace allows Him not only to forgive, but even to forget your trespass.

Guidance

That he lavished on us with all wisdom and understanding. And he made known to us the mystery of his will according to his good pleasure, which he purposed in Christ, to be put into effect when the times will have reached their fulfillment—to bring all things in heaven and on earth together under one head, even Christ.

—Romans 1:8-10

When you receive Christ, you are no longer alone as you try to figure out the mystery of God's will. The Holy Spirit will never lead you astray. He's better than your own personal GPS, because He not only gives direction— He tells you the best place to go.

The Feeling of Forgiveness

Guilt

On three occasions Simon Peter betrayed Jesus Christ:

A servant girl saw him seated there in the firelight. She looked closely at him and said, "This man was with him." But he denied it. "Woman, I don't know him," he said. A little later someone else saw him and said, "You also are one of them." "Man, I am not!" Peter replied. About an hour later another asserted, "Certainly this fellow was with him, for he is a Galilean." Peter replied, "Man, I don't know what you're talking about!" Just as he was speaking, the rooster crowed. The Lord turned and looked straight at Peter. Then Peter remembered the word the Lord had spoken to him: "Before the rooster crows today, you will disown me three times." And he went outside and wept bitterly.

—Luke 22:56-62

Peter's guilt and shame weighed heavily on his mind. He knew he had betrayed the one he loved—the very Son of God. You don't just get over that. That kind of shame sticks.

Sometimes, our shame sticks even when we're considered to be heroes. Chelsey "Sully" Sullenberger is the pilot who successfully ditched US Airways Flight 1549 in the Hudson River off Manhattan, New York City, on January 15, 2009, saving the lives of all 155 people on the aircraft. Far from feeling like a hero, the trauma caused Sullenberger to say: "One of the hardest things for me to do in this whole experience was to forgive myself for not having done something else."

We know what guilt feels like.

- *Guilt destroys our confidence.* Jesus replied, "I tell you the truth, if you have faith and do not doubt, not only can you do what was done to the fig tree, but also you can say to this mountain, 'Go, throw yourself into the sea,' and it will be done" (Matthew 21:21).
- *Guilt damages our relationships.* "If we confess our sins, he is faithful and just and will forgive us our sins and purify us from all unrighteousness" (1 John 1:9).
- *Guilt defeats our faith.* But when he asks, he must believe and not doubt, because he who doubts is like a wave of the sea, blown and tossed by the wind (James 1:6).

Restoration

Peter's restoration may be one of the most beautiful stories in the Bible (though I admit there are many contenders). After Jesus is resurrected, He appears to Peter and asks three times if Peter loves Him. Jesus knew the answer, but He gave Peter the opportunity to express his love as many times as he had denied his Lord. If anyone had reason to shout from the rooftops how glorious forgiveness is, it's Peter.

> Peter replied, "Repent and be baptized, every one of you, in the name of Jesus Christ for the forgiveness of your sins. And you will receive the gift of the Holy Spirit."
>
> —Acts 2:38

The apostle Paul, who had tormented and persecuted Christians, also knew the power of forgiveness: "I'm a debtor. I will spend the rest of my life in complete devotion to Christ." As a result, He experienced the joy of forgiveness, the help of God and the protection of God.

> Brothers, I do not consider myself yet to have taken hold of it. But one thing I do: Forgetting what is behind and straining toward what is ahead.
>
> —Philippians 3:13

One of the all-time greats in baseball was Babe Ruth. His bat had the power of a cannon, and his record of 714 home runs remained unbroken until Hank Aaron came along. The Babe was the idol of sports fans, but in time age took its toll, and his popularity began to wane. Finally, the Yankees traded him to the Braves. In one of his last games in Cincinnati, Babe Ruth began to falter. He struck out and made several misplays that allowed the Reds to score five runs in one inning. As the Babe walked toward the dugout, chin down and dejected, there rose from the stands an enormous storm of boos and catcalls. Some fans actually shook their fists. Then a wonderful thing happened. A little boy jumped over the railing, and with tears streaming down his cheeks he ran out to the great athlete. Unashamedly, he flung his arms around the Babe's legs and held on tightly. Babe Ruth scooped him up, hugged him, and set him down again. Patting him gently on the head, he took his hand and the two of them walked off the field together.[17]

Jesus is a friend who loves you in spite of your faults and failures.

---

[17]Source Unknown.

3

God Can Deliver Me
Even Quicker Than
Next Day Air

So we say with confidence,
"The Lord is my helper; I will not
be afraid. What can man do to me?"

—Hebrews 13:5–6

Kumar, a Christian in South India, was grieved because none of the thirteen people he had invited had come to watch a Billy Graham television special at his home on December 23. He began to pray, and around 9:00 p.m. he felt compelled to invite his wife's sister's family to watch the next night's broadcast.

The family had no phone, so Kumar asked a neighbor to bring them to the phone for an urgent message. When his brother-in-law, Satish, reached the phone, Kumar asked him and his family to catch a bus to the city. Satish said he had no money. Kumar encouraged him to borrow the money and said that he would reimburse Satish for the tickets.

Satish consented, and at 4:00 a.m. he and his family boarded a bus for the long trip to Kumar's house. They arrived at 5:00 p.m., and an hour later they watched the *My Hope* telecast from the Billy Graham Evangelistic Association. Afterward, Kumar gave his testimony and asked if the others wanted to put their faith in Christ. They were all looking at each other, and Kumar wondered why. Then Satish, noticeably distressed, stood and explained that he had lost his job because the tea factory he worked for had closed. Further, the company was demanding that the family vacate their company-owned house. Seeing no hope, the family had decided that on December 25 they were all going to commit suicide.

Now they saw they had hope in Jesus, so they prayed with Kumar to accept Christ. Satish said he felt like a new man. After staying several more days with Kumar, the family returned home ready to face the future with Christ.[18]

Christianity is a religion of hope. The Bible reminds us that Christ is the only hope for our desperate world.

Because we have heard of your faith in Christ Jesus and of the love you have for all the saints—the faith and love that spring from the hope that is stored up for you in heaven and that you have already heard about in the word of truth, the gospel that has come to you. All over the world this gospel is bearing fruit and growing, just as it has been doing among you since the day you heard it and understood God's grace in all its truth.

—Colossians 1:4-6

By the power of Jesus, we are delivered.

Bondage

To Despair

Despair is the complete lack of hope—an awful, god-forsaken place to be. Sometimes our circumstances are so utterly devastating that we plunge into the pit of despair with great angst, believing that life will never be good again. Other times we slip into despair due to boredom,

---

[18]Bob Paulson, "My Hope: India," Decision (March 2006).

loss of interest in life, depression, loneliness—without even trying to escape. Either way, our separation from God is what makes despair so miserable.

Despair enslaves us. It sucks our energy and joy while tightening our bonds. Sometimes when we're in despair, we know we want out, but we're helpless to deliver ourselves. Sometimes we actually get used to the feeling of despair and don't even know we want out anymore. Sometimes we've been in despair for as long as we can remember, and we don't even know we're being held captive—in other words, we don't know that God is not with us.

Without Christ, there is no hope—and despair is a real thing.

Once we know Him and are lifted out of the pit, we experience a freedom we hadn't even dreamed about. It's like tasting cheesecake for the first time, or experiencing your first snowfall, or falling in love—only much better! You didn't know how wonderful it would be; but now that you do, you'll never go back.

> Remember that at that time you were separate from Christ, excluded from citizenship in Israel and foreigners to the covenants of the promise, without hope and without God in the world.
>
> —Ephesians 2:12

To False Gods

Salvation is found in Christ alone. When we give our hearts to other gods, we put ourselves in bondage.

He then brought them out and asked, "Sirs, what must I do to be saved?" They replied, "Believe in the Lord Jesus, and you will be saved—you and your household.

—Acts 16:30-31

It's not likely that anyone reading this book will go out and buy a wooden statue to pray to. Our modern-day gods usually come in other forms—anything that we love or trust more than we trust God. We might not tithe because we trust those dollars in our bank account more than the God who provides the money in the first place. We might skip an opportunity to worship God to attend an opportunity to worship our favorite rock star or sports team. We might neglect to live for Christ to win the approval of another person.

The problem with worshiping other gods is that we are selecting the wrong master. Money can disappear in an instant, even if you've been financially astute all your life—or it can consume you and turn you into a greedy, unloving person. A pop star or sports hero might go down in the hall of fame, but they don't know your name; your love is empty, unrewarded, meaningless. And other people, no matter how wonderful they are, will eventually let you down. Perhaps even if God placed these people in your life for your mutual benefit, they can never meet all your needs.

False gods can do nothing but separate you from God and put you in bondage.

All that changes when we make Jesus Lord of our lives! He alone sets us free, gives us meaning, and loves us purely.

Yet to all who received him, to those who believed in his name, he gave the right to become children of God.

—John 1:12

To Self

Sometimes we're in bondage to ourselves.

What a wretched man I am! Who will rescue me from this body of death?

—Romans 7:24

We might have an ego the size of Texas, and think we can do no wrong. We won't rely on anyone but ourselves, and will never put others first. We have no idea that making "me" the most important thing to self makes us unimportant, and unappealing, to others.

Others have an inferiority complex, and pander to the needs of others—but only in an attempt to win their approval. We have put ourselves at the center of the universe as much as the egomaniac has, with the same effect.

Either way, we may entirely fool ourselves into thinking this is normal, or right, or effective, or inevitable.

The heart is deceitful above all things and beyond cure. Who can understand it? "I the LORD search the heart and examine the mind, to reward a man according to his conduct, according to what his deeds deserve."

—Jeremiah 17:9-10

Thankfully, God can save us even from ourselves. He is the God of truth and wisdom, and He will open our eyes if we really want to see. He will humble us, and lift us up again.

To inoculate me from the praise of man,
He baptized me in the criticism of man,
until I died to the control of man.

—Francis Frangipane

To Legalism

I know some folks who maintain strong family values, and I applaud them. They keep a close eye on every internet site their children visit. They listen to only Christian music and they read only Christian books. They understand the importance of filling their minds with pure and godly messages, knowing that we are shaped by what we hear. The benefits of this life choice are beautiful, even though maintaining such standards is difficult. he kids are passionate about their faith and living godly lives, and the parents too are mature Christians.

It was interesting to me, then, that the wife began having doubts about their choice. "When I noticed my daughter was judging another girl for watching a certain movie, I realized something was wrong. That other little girl was clearly in love with the Lord as well, but all my daughter could see was what she was doing wrong." The parents wisely began to speak to their children about spiritual pride and legalism. "While I still strongly believe we are making the right choices, it will be all for nothing if we get eaten up by pride, she reasoned."

The law matters! Living according to God's standards is important. But when we start worshipping the law rather than walking with Christ, we are in danger of failing altogether. Our good behavior doesn't get us to heaven.

Know that a man is not justified by observing the law, but by faith in Jesus Christ. So we, too, have put our faith in Christ Jesus that we may be justified by faith in Christ and not by observing the law, because by observing the law no one will be justified.
—Galatians 2:16

We could live our lives as the Pharisees did—studying the law day and night, following every rule down to the letter, enforcing these standards on everyone else. But that's not what God wants from us. He has set us free from living that way!

Before this faith came, we were held prisoners by the law, locked up until faith should be revealed. So the law was put in charge to lead us to Christ that we might be justified by faith. Now that faith has come, we are no longer under the supervision of the law.
—Galatians 3:23-25

Legalism, according to Webster is a "strict, often too strict and literal, adherence to law or to a code." Thank you, Jesus, for saving us from that kind of bondage!

To Moralism

Sometimes I hear people talking about a certain area of town or a certain region of the country or a certain school district as having good Christian values. While I certainly appreciate and encourage decency, I don't want us to get mixed up about what Christians are. We are not a political party, we are not a social club, and neither are we the morality police.

Yes, we are called to live righteously (which includes both refraining from unholy acts and participating in holy ones; i.e., don't get drunk and do feed the hungry), but our primary task is to introduce others to Christ. If our focus as Christians is to be nice people and to surround ourselves with nice people, it's very possible we'll forget to mention Christ at all.

> For through the law I died to the law so that I might live for God.
>
> —Galatians 2:19

To Ritualism

I know a family that follows professional football passionately. They have a great time with it—gathering together every weekend to watch their team, donning their jerseys proudly, participating in friendly banter with anyone who will engage. They are godly people (who happen to be just as passionate about serving at the church), which makes it all the more fun to tease them about their football rituals. If their team won the opening game, they have to turn the TV on exactly twelve minutes before kickoff for every game after, just as they did on that first game. They have to eat the same food, they have to wear the same jerseys (not even washing them for fear of washing off that good luck). They even have to keep the dog outside or inside, depending on where the poor creature was on that opening game.

I don't know where this family came up with their crazy ideas, but they seem to think their rituals work. I think this activity is harmless fun for them, a way to feel like they are participating with their beloved team, but I am reminded of how we as Christians can get caught up in our rituals; thinking if we only do *this* right or *that* right, everything will go exactly as we want it to. Just as that football family seems to take credit for the win rather than applauding the players, we think we're the ones who are saving ourselves rather than thanking God for His grace. We recite the right creed, we attend church without fail, we tithe faithfully, we serve at vacation Bible school and tell the children Bible stories—but we neglect authentic worship.

Here is what the bondage of ritualism looks like:

Hypocritically, professing belief, performing rote rituals, calling oneself a member of religion without attempting to follow holy prescriptive, participating in church with a social holy country-club fervor—these can all be an evasion of holy duty, yet another form of idolatry, as practicing the "religion" becomes its own end point.[19]

---

[19]Laura Schlessinger, Ten Commandments, pg. 60.

Listen to what God says:

"I hate, I despise your religious feasts;
I cannot stand your assemblies.
Even though you bring me burnt offerings and
    grain offerings,
I will not accept them.
Though you bring choice fellowship offerings,
I will have no regard for them.
Away with the noise of your songs!
I will not listen to the music of your harps.
But let justice roll on like a river,
righteousness like a never-failing stream!"
—Amos 5:21-24

Steps to Deliverance

Until that glorious day when we will meet our Lord, our deliverance is incomplete. But even here on earth we can be delivered—not yet from death, but from other things that Satan would like to overload us with.

Through Confession

Confession is one of those things that sounds easy to do, but is impossible to achieve without the right heart. True confession requires us to be broken.

Mike, who works with homeless people, told Philip Yancy that those who have hit bottom don't waste time building up an image or trying to conform. And they pray without pretense, a refreshing contrast to what is found in some churches. When Yancy asked for an example,

God Can Do Anything But Fail

Mike said, "My friend and I were playing guitars and singing 'As the Deer Panteth for the Water' when David, a homeless man, started weeping. 'That's what I want, man,' he said. 'I want that water. I'm an alcoholic, and I want to be healed.'"[20]

Confession isn't just throwing in one line during an unfeeling prayer: "And please forgive my sins." Confession is admitting to God in all sincerity that you have done wrong, and that you desperately need Him. It is naming your sin, and humbly begging for mercy and healing.

> But if we walk in the light, as he is in the light, we have fellowship with one another, and the blood of Jesus, his Son, purifies us from all sin. If we claim to be without sin, we deceive ourselves and the truth is not in us. If we confess our sins, he is faithful and just and will forgive us our sins and purify us from all unrighteousness.
>
> —1 John 1:7-9

Through Cleansing

Bob Beasley, a pastor in Chatham, Ontario, tells the story of Rena, age three, who sat with him during a baptismal service, which was a new experience for her. "Why did Pastor Bob push that guy in the water?" she asked.

Bob's wife quietly tried to explain, but Rena wasn't satisfied. Later that night they tried again. They talked about sin and how, when people decide to live for Jesus and "do good," they want everyone to know. They explained that

God Can Deliver Me Even Quicker Than Next Day Air

---

[20]Philip Yancey, "The Word on the Street," Christianity Today (January 2006).

water symbolizes Jesus' washing away people's sin; when they come out "clean," they will try to be "good."

A moment later, Bob and his wife realized they'd failed again when Rena asked, "Why didn't Pastor Bob just spank him?"

Spiritual cleansing is hard to understand, no matter what age we are. It seems like confession should be enough. What more is needed?

Scripture is clear: "Since we have these promises, dear friends, let us purify ourselves from everything that contaminates body and spirit, perfecting holiness out of reverence for God" (2 Corinthians 7:1).

One definition of sanctification goes like this:

> We believe that entire sanctification is that act of God, subsequent to regeneration, by which believers are made free from original sin, or depravity, and brought into a state of entire devotement to God and the holy obedience of love made perfect.[21]

Baptism is a symbol of sanctification, a ritual given to us by God—and one that has been deeply meaningful for many people over the centuries. But heart purity is at the center of our sanctification. Baptism is just the tool. The objective is to die to self—to destroy the sinful nature—so that you can be clothed in robes of righteousness.

> For God has not called us unto uncleanness, but unto holiness.
>
> —1 Thessalonians 4:7 KJV

---

[21]Manual, Church of the Nazarene, Article 10.

Into Confidence

We aren't tossed from the frying pan into the fire when we are delivered from ourselves. We are brought into God's kingdom.

Redemption does something to a person. It gives the most timid person inexplicable confidence. Lloyd Ogilvie says, "The most powerful historical proof of the resurrection is the 'resurrected' disciples. Dull, defeated people became fearless, adventuresome leaders. Cowards became courageous; the timid become bold."

It's like we have this secret. We know something that others may not, something that changes everything. We're like a person who holds a gun to their head, but who happens to know there are no bullets loaded. Or the person who goes back in time and invests in a dot com, even though personal computers are almost non-existent. Or like the boy who asks out a girl after finding her diary that she had written all about him. That secret gives you confidence that others may not understand.

> "But you will receive power when the Holy Spirit comes on you; and you will be my witnesses in Jerusalem, and in all Judea and Samaria, and to the ends of the earth."
>
> —Acts 1:8

People everywhere are bound by addictive behaviors and the bondage of Satan. Paul emphasizes that deliverance is available to every believer. In fact, through Christ, anyone can become "free at last!" Freedom is usually associated with your birthright or acceptance as an American citizen. But Paul points out that only in Christ Jesus are people set free.

Eternal Deliverance

Some might ask what exactly we're saved from when we're born again. It's a fair question. We're saved from eternal death.

I don't mean to be a flaming fire and brimstone preachers, but I'm not going to avoid saying the truth either. Separation from God isn't like getting caffeine-free soda rather than the real stuff; it's not like sitting in coach rather than first class; it's not like getting a pet fish rather than a dog. It's like getting fired instead of a promotion, being hated by the girl of your dreams instead of loved, having multiple miscarriages instead of a large family. Only much worse—and the gnawing pain lasts forever.

What are we saved from? We're saved from eternal death, eternal separation from God, eternal despair. Instead, we're given new life, eternal life, joy-filled communion with our Heavenly Father.

[God] has saved us and called us to a holy life—not because of anything we have done but because of his own purpose and grace. This grace was given us in Christ Jesus before the beginning of time, but it has now been revealed through the appearing of our Savior, Christ Jesus, who has destroyed death and has brought life and immortality to light through the gospel.

—2 Timothy 1:9–10

How is this possible? Can we really be saved simply by confessing our sins? What's the "deep magic" behind our immortality?

Our eternal salvation is made possible because Jesus Christ, the Son of God, perfect and without sin, freely gave His life to pay for our sins, and rose from the dead to reign forever. All we have to do is accept the gift of grace.

Not that accepting the gift is easy. It takes humility, and submission, and genuine heart change, and disgust for our cherished vices, and hunger for renewal. Accepting grace is as weighty as accepting a marriage proposal, even more so. It's not as risky though. A marriage partner may fail you (or vise verse), but God never will. He's never going away, He'll never quit loving you. He will never abandon you.

In the book *Lead to Succeed* Jerry and I tell the story of an airplane that faced sudden turbulence. The copilot walked into the passenger section and explained that they were having a problem with one of the engines, but he assured them that the other three engines were working. As he went back to the cockpit he suddenly turned around and said, "Oh, I almost forgot. You'll also be relieved to know that we have three pastors on board this flight."

One of the passengers turned to another and said, "I don't know about you, but I'd just as soon have four good engines."

Considering that I could have been one of those pastors, I don't blame the guy.

All kidding aside, let me tell you that I'd just as soon have my Rock and my Redeemer on board. Four working engines are much less reliable than the immortal God. The plane may go down, but I'd just point to Jesus and say, "I'm with Him."

Bruce Larson said, "The events of Easter cannot be reduced to a creed or philosophy. We are not asked to believe the doctrine of the resurrection. We are asked to meet this person raised from the dead. In faith, we move from belief in a doctrine to a knowledge of a person. Ultimate truth is a person. We met Him. He is alive."

> For the Lord himself will come down from heaven, with a loud command, with the voice of the archangel and with the trumpet call of God, and the dead in Christ will rise first.
>
> —1 Thessalonians 4:16

Immortality! What thrills me most about the idea of living forever is not the idea of being alive forever— after living more than half a century, forever sounds like a long time. What's exciting is that I'll be transformed in the twinkling of an eye—transformed so completely that I'll be able to approach the throne of God and spend eternity with Him.

> The faith and love that spring from the hope that is stored up for you in heaven and that you have already heard about in the word of truth, the gospel.
>
> —Colossians 1:5

Deliverance into Love

God has more for you. He has delivered you from bondage into His family. You are now his son or daughter.

Enabled to Mature

God has given you everything you need to grow into the person He wants you to be. You may stumble from time to time, but He'll lift you up and help you finish the race.

> He who began a good work in you will carry it on to completion until the day of Christ Jesus.
> —Philippians 1:6

You have to do your part, of course. Read the Word, pray, give, witness, love. You can't be like the middle-schooler who says to her parents after getting poor marks in school, "I'm trying as hard as I can!"—without doing any homework, without studying, and without participating in class. Trying is not gritting your teeth, clenching your fists, and saying, "I can do this." Trying is putting effort into the steps that lead to success.

If you want to mature in Christ, you have to surrender all you have and all you are to Him every single day.

Empowered to Serve

When we are in bondage to ourselves, our world is small. It's all about us. When we are set free, God opens our eyes to see others, to make a difference in the world, to touch lives.

It's true there are plenty of do-gooders out there who don't know the Lord—and their work is still effective and good. I once thanked a woman for her ministry, only to have her reply curtly that her organization was *not* a ministry. I'm still glad for her ministry (because in fact she is ministering to people), but I'm very sad she's missing out on the joy of the Lord and the empowerment of the Spirit. Imagine how much more she could do if she would hand the reigns over to the Lord?

> So he said to me, "This is the word of the LORD to Zerubbabel: 'Not by might nor by power, but by my Spirit,' says the LORD Almighty."
> —Zechariah 4:6

When we are delivered, born again, saved—or whatever term you'd like to use—you discover how powerful God is. We are not limited by your own skills, experiences, or resources. Your humanitarian efforts come in line with God's great love for His people, and fireworks go off.

> Are you so foolish? After beginning with the Spirit, are you now trying to attain your goal by human effort?
> —Galatians 3:3

Energized to Live

Freedom fighter Patrick Henry once said as a delegate to the First Continental Congress, "Give me liberty or give me death." The last paragraph of his will is on display in the Brookneal, Virginia County Courthouse. "I have now given everything I own to my children. There is one more thing I wish I could give them and that is Christ. Because if they have everything I gave them and don't have Christ they have nothing."

I have been crucified with Christ and I no longer live, but Christ lives in me. The life I live in the body, I live by faith in the Son of God, who loved me and gave himself for me.

—Galatians 2:20

God Can Heal Me Even

When The Doctor Shakes Her

Head and Walks Away

For I am poor and needy, and my heart is wounded within me.

—Psalm 109:22

On a Sunday morning in January 2006, five young men attacked and threatened to kill a Protestant church leader in Turkey. Kamil Kiroglu, twenty-nine, had just left his church in Adana when he was ambushed and beaten so severely that he fell unconscious twice.

"They were trying to force me to deny Jesus," Kiroglu said. "But each time they asked me to deny Jesus and become a Muslim, I said, 'Jesus is Lord.' The more I said, 'Jesus is Lord,' the more they beat me." One of the attackers pulled out a long knife and threatened to kill Kiroglu if he did not deny his Christian faith and return to Islam. Kiroglu refused.

After the incident, he said, "I am praising God—not because he saved me from death, but because he helped me not to deny him in the shadow of death."[22]

This is a chapter on healing; but before we can dig into the thrill of knowing God can heal us, we have to look closely at our motives. Do we, like Kiroglu, have faith so real that we're willing to be hurt rather than healed? Because that's what it's going to take.

---

[22] "Convert Christian Beaten Unconscious," Compass Direct (January 20, 2006).

Blind Faith

Our Condition

We all have wounds, whether physical or otherwise—and we all need healing. Let's take a look at a story of Jesus encountering one man who, like us, needed healing.

> As he went along, he saw a man blind from birth. His disciples asked him, "Rabbi, who sinned, this man or his parents, that he was born blind?" "Neither this man nor his parents sinned," said Jesus, "but this happened so that the work of God might be displayed in his life. As long as it is day, we must do the work of him who sent me. Night is coming, when no one can work."
>
> —John 9:1-4

Imagine the helplessness this man must have felt as a blind person. He would not have been able to earn a living, start a family, or even hope for improvement in his condition. He was entirely dependent on others, all the while having to endure their scorn. The disciples assumed that he had some spiritual deficiency—that he was born that way because of some sin in his life or in his parents' life. Jesus knew better. He gave them something to look forward to.

I love the Peanut's cartoon where Lucy and Linus are watching TV.

Lucy: "Go get me a glass of water."

Linus: "Why should I do anything for you? You never do anything for me."

Lucy: "I promise that I will bake you a cake on your 75th birthday."

Linus, as he gets up and goes into the kitchen: "Life is more pleasant when you have something to look forward to."

Hope opens the door to a touch from God. When we believe that good things will happen, they can happen. Our hopeful faith is the key to unlocking God's riches.

The Compassion of Jesus

"While I am in the world, I am the light of the world." Having said this, he spit on the ground, made some mud with the saliva, and put it on the man's eyes. "Go," he told him, "wash in the Pool of Siloam" (this word means Sent). So the man went and washed, and came home seeing.

—John 9:5-7

A Healing Touch. Jesus could have pulled diamonds from the air to replace the old, broken pair of eyes the blind man had been carrying around all these years; He could have stood back with both hands outstretched, shooting bolts of light from his fingertips to the man's face; He could have spoken in a voice so loud and mighty that everyone in the vicinity would tremble—but Jesus didn't. His healing touch was quiet, earthy, simple.

It reminds me of the story of a young girl who was suffering from anorexia and bulimia, and was undergoing treatment at Baptist Medical Center in Kansas City. On a particularly difficult day she was told to drink a glass of milk, but she just couldn't. Her doctor was called in. He sat down beside her on the bed and said, "You are a Christian, correct?" When she answered yes, he said, "Do you remember the man Jesus healed near the pool of Siloam? Jesus put mud on his eyes to bring about his healing. But what really healed him?"

She thought for a moment and then answered, "His faith."

"Good!" he said. "Now drink your mud."[23]

A Transforming Touch. A touch from Jesus is always life-altering, no matter how mundane the process. The impossible happens. We are changed in ways we hadn't imagined. The man in this story, who hadn't seen even a shadow as long as he had lived, could suddenly cast his eyes upon the faces of his parents, his home, the trees and birds and rivers. He was healed!

The Toler family is not a stranger to God's healing touch. From my son Adam's healing from a life-threatening infection shortly after he was born to my wife Linda's battle with cancer, and now being pronounced cancer free, we have known the awesome power of God to bring deliverance from disease and pain.

A few years back I was in Portland, Maine, for a speaking engagement. My host, Dr. Wayne Brewer, picked me up at the airport and was taking me out to eat with our mutual friend Dr. Jimmy Smith. We were stopped at a red light, when suddenly a 16-year-old driver talking on a cell phone proved scientifically that a Ford Explorer will fit in the back of a Dodge Caravan. Unfortunately, I

[23]Steve T., Florence, Kansas.

was seated in the rear passenger seat of the van. After the unscheduled meeting of the two vehicles and the usual "Is everyone all right?" I realized I had suffered an injury to my shoulder.

Not long after the Portland car accident, I went to see a surgeon and was scheduled to have rotator cuff surgery. A few days before my scheduled operation, I flew to Alaska to speak. The flight home was a bit of a challenge since I couldn't raise my right arm above my waist (which makes it even more difficult to stuff a suitcase in the overhead bin of the plane). Further, I arrived late in Dallas and missed my flight to Oklahoma City. Renting a car in Dallas and driving to Oklahoma City with a 4:00 a.m. arrival didn't give me much "beauty sleep," but I was up at 7:00 a.m. and went to church to meet my prayer partners and focus on the morning message.

After the prayer time I noticed I had an e-mail from my friend Bill Burch that was titled "My Never Again List." One of the scripture verses in the list was from Isaiah 53:5, "By His stripes I am healed." Since I was preaching on the Wisdom of Words that morning, I quickly printed the e-mail and took it with me to the pulpit.

The lack of sleep combined with a super size jet lag affected my sermon introduction in a rather embarrassing way. I said, "This morning I want to speak on the subject of incest." I tried to recover, "No, I don't mean 'incest'. . . I mean I want to speak on 'incest.'" After the third try (with the same results) I finally said above the laughter of the audience, "WILL SOMEONE HELP ME . . . WHAT ARE THOSE CREATURES THAT CRAWL ON THE EARTH AND WORK TOGETHER AS TEAMS?!"

A thousand people answered as one: "INSECTS!" I said, "*THAT'S* WHAT I WANT TO SPEAK ON TODAY!"

As I moved into the heart of the message, I reached a point where I pulled out the "Never Again List" from my friend and began to read the verses. When I read the Isaiah passage "By His stripes I am healed . . ." my right arm (with the injured shoulder) went straight up in the air. Instantly I knew that God had healed me.

That week the surgery that had been planned was cancelled and since then I haven't had a pain in that shoulder. God had touched me—and just at a time when I needed a sign from above that He was at work in my church and in my life.

A Freeing Touch. Being healed by Jesus changes more than the physical body. Our spiritual eyes are opened, and we are set free to experience God in a whole new way.

Wayne Messmer, an announcer and singer for sports teams in the Windy City, could tell you the truth of this statement. After singing "The Star-Spangled Banner" at a Chicago Blackhawks game in 1994, Messmer was shot by two teenage boys. The bullet passed through the singer's throat, so doctors weren't sure if Messmer would sing again. Amazingly, six months later, Messmer returned to the microphone.

Physical healing was one thing; emotional release of the hatred and resentment he felt was another. For that, Messmer had to trust Christ, his Savior, to help him reach the point where he could forgive his shooters. When he did, he found freedom. As he says in *The Voice of Victory*, "Over a period of contemplative and reflective prayer and meditation, I was confident I had set myself free from the chains that had connected me to the incident."

Although one of the boys had been released on a plea bargain, the other, James Hampton, was still in jail. To prove that he truly had forgiven his would-be killers, Messmer drove 225 miles to Galesburg Correctional Center and asked to see Hampton.

Several years had passed, but Messmer found the grace to say, "James, I'm here to see how you are doing." After a two-hour emotional visit, Messmer turned to leave. Reaching out and touching Hampton's forearm, he offered a benediction: "James, I bid you peace."[24]

I have a feeling the person who was truly given peace at that moment was Messmer. When God touches, we are able to see at a higher level, and we are set free.

The Blindness of Others

Sometimes when we have been set free, the people around us are still blind. God may have opened our eyes, but He works on each of us in his own time, in his own way, and we can't expect everyone to be where we are.

His neighbors and those who had formerly seen him begging asked, "Isn't this the same man who used to sit and beg?" Some claimed that he was. Others said, "No, he only looks like him." But he himself insisted, "I am the man." "How then were your eyes opened?" they demanded. He replied, "The man they call Jesus made some mud and put

---

[24]Pat Karlak, "Messmer Writes of Recovery, Forgiveness," *Daily Herald*, Arlington Heights, Illinois ?(January 16, 2000).

it on my eyes. He told me to go to Siloam and wash. So I went and washed, and then I could see." "Where is this man?" they asked him. "I don't know," he said. They brought to the Pharisees the man who had been blind. Now the day on which Jesus had made the mud and opened the man's eyes was a Sabbath. Therefore the Pharisees also asked him how he had received his sight. "He put mud on my eyes," the man replied, "and I washed, and now I see." Some of the Pharisees said, "This man is not from God, for he does not keep the Sabbath." But others asked, "How can a sinner do such miraculous signs?" So they were divided.

—John 9:8-16

Clearly, the man who had been healed was not the one who was actually blind. It was the others who were blind spiritually speaking!

The disciples were blinded by prejudice. Even Jesus' closest companions could not see what Jesus saw. The disciples saw a beggar, one tainted by sin ("Who sinned, this man or his parent?"). Jesus saw a man who needed healing.

The neighbors doubted. Skeptics will always be with us, no matter how obvious the miracle.

The Pharisees attacked Christ by saying He was not of God (v. 16) and calling Him a sinner (v. 24). The son told what he knew (v. 25) and showed the Pharisees how foolish their thinking was (vv. 30-33). The simple-hearted believer knows more spiritual truth than unsaved educated theologians. Jesus gave him eyesight *and* insight.

His parents were frightened. The religious leaders had let it be known that anyone who confessed Christ openly would be cast out of the synagogue (v. 22). This meant, of course, losing friends and family and all the benefits of the Jewish religion. It was this declaration that forced the blind man's parents and neighbors to "beat around the bush" when asked about his amazing cure. The son's simple confession in v. 11 exalted Christ. The final result: they excommunicated the man from the synagogue.

It would have been easy for the son to hide his confession and thus avoid controversy, but he fearlessly stood his ground. He knew what a difference Christ had made in his life, and he could not deny it. Everyone who has met Christ and trusted Him should make it known openly.

—Warren Werisbe

If you have been given spiritual sight, thank God for the gift. It is only by the Spirit that you are able to see. Those around you need your love and patience and guidance.

Divine Power

"Is any one of you in trouble? He should pray. Is anyone happy? Let him sing songs of praise. Is any one of you sick? He should call the elders of the church to pray over him and anoint him with oil in the name of the Lord. And the prayer offered in faith will make the sick person well; the Lord will raise him up. If he has sinned, he will be forgiven."

—James 5:13–15

Understanding God's Healing

First, God heals through the natural process. Whether we're dealing with a bad cold, teenage angst, the pain of loss, or financial instability, waiting will often be the primary agent in healing. Taking right and careful steps during this time certainly assists the process, but desperate appeals for divine intervention will probably not help. Believe it or not, God may be trying to heal your true ailment, which requires time. They say time is the great healer—and God is the Creator of time.

God also heals through the hands of a skilled surgeon. I am constantly amazed by the wonders of modern science. What our doctors, nurses, hospitals, and medicines can do today is astonishing. Even the things that seem so simple to us—like a pair of glasses or a bottle of antibiotics—are nothing short of miraculous. Just imagine life without them, and you will know what I mean. My wife Linda and I will always be thankful for God's provision in this way. We are forever indebted to Dr. Michael Santi who operated on Linda for colon cancer in 1991. His skill, confident faith and prayer before the surgery gave us the strength that we needed to endure. Today Linda remains cancer free. Thanks to God for His touch and for good doctors like Dr. Santi.

God heals through the miraculous intervention in our lives as well. This kind of healing is more rare, but it does still happen today. Tyler Clarensau, a 15-year-old boy with malformed knee joints that caused swelling and great pain, took a risk and went to the altar to ask for healing. Forty other young people circled him and prayed, and soon the whole congregation joined in until someone boldly announced that God had healed the boy. Tyler shakily stood up, then did deep knee bends—something he hadn't accomplished in years. Today he can walk— even run. "I'd heard about people getting healed," he says. "I thought it was pretty cool. But I didn't know for sure about such healing until it happened to me."[25]

Recognizing Your Miracle

To receive your miracle, you must recognize Jesus Christ as your healer. No matter how your healing comes about—whether through an obvious divine intervention or a more subtle act of God—give credit to the Healer. I'm not like a high school English teacher trying to teach you of the importance of never plagiarizing; I'm like the coach telling you to keep your eye on the ball. Recognizing that Jesus is your healer is for your sake more than His. He's not going to change, whether or not you acknowledge Him; but you will be changed if you stay focused on Him.

Jesus Christ is the same yesterday and today and forever.

—Hebrews 13:8

To recognize your healing, you must believe that He is able to heal you. Before J. Oswald Sanders was fifty, he had arthritis so bad that he could hardly get out of

[25]Kenneth Woodward, "Should You Believe in Miracles?" Newsweek (May 1, 2000).

bed. He could have taken a nice retirement. Instead, he entered the most productive years of his life. At age fifty, he left a prosperous career as an attorney in New Zealand to lead the China Inland Mission (now Overseas Missionary Fellowship). After several years of leading the mission, he retired, only to take on the directorship of a Christian college. Then he retired again. As a two-time widower, he certainly deserved a rest. But rather than taking it easy, he accelerated, spending his last twenty years speaking around the world more than three hundred times per year. His respect grew even though he never sought the limelight or tried to maintain his position. He was almost ninety and working on a book when he died.[26]

> "For I know the plans I have for you," declares the LORD, "plans to prosper you and not to harm you, plans to give you hope and a future."
> —Jeremiah 29:11

To recognize your healing, you must ask God to heal you now! Asking God to heal you is risky, isn't it? It seems like such a simple thing to do, but there is so much behind the asking. What if He doesn't heal you? Will you begin doubting? What if He does heal you? Will you have to make changes after witnessing such an audacious miracle? Remove the spotlight from yourself for a moment, and ask God what *He* wants for you.

God Can Do Anything But Fail

---

[26]Jerry White, Dangers ?Men Face (NavPress, 1997)

You want something but don't get it. You kill and covet, but you cannot have what you want. You quarrel and fight. You do not have, because you do not ask God.

—James 4:2

When you recognize your healing, you must testify to it. Actually, testifying to a great thing that has happened to you is a natural response.

A medical missionary served many years in India in a region where there was progressive blindness. People were born with healthy vision, but something in that area caused people to lose their sight as they matured. This missionary had developed a process that would arrest progressive blindness, so people came to him for this transforming operation. Interestingly, the people never said, "Thank you," because that phrase was not in their dialect. Instead, they spoke a word that meant, "I will tell your name." Wherever they went, they would tell the name of the missionary who had cured their blindness. They had received something so wonderful that they eagerly proclaimed it.[27]

True Healing

Verbalizing Your Need

Another story in Scripture teaches us what true healing is. Jesus was on His way to a feast in Jerusalem. En route to the feast, He came upon the Pool of Siloam. It appears

[27]Source: SermonCentral Staff. Citations: Melvin Newland, Central Christian Church

from a Bible study perspective that many people with disabilities were placed by the pool seeking to be healed.

> Some time later, Jesus went up to Jerusalem for a feast of the Jews. Now there is in Jerusalem near the Sheep Gate a pool, which in Aramaic is called Bethesda and which is surrounded by five covered colonnades. Here a great number of disabled people used to lie—the blind, the lame, the paralyzed. One who was there had been an invalid for thirty-eight years. When Jesus saw him lying there and learned that he had been in this condition for a long time, he asked him, "Do you want to get well?" "Sir," the invalid replied, "I have no one to help me into the pool when the water is stirred. While I am trying to get in, someone else goes down ahead of me.
>
> —John 5:1-7

Jesus wanted the man to verbalize his need. Jesus seems to ask the obvious here. Who wouldn't want to be cured from such a terrible condition? That Jesus was prompting the man to state his need is consistent with the rest of Scripture: God knows what we need, but He still asks us to pray.

> "Your Father knows what you need before you ask him."
>
> —Matthew 6:8

Jesus wanted him to increase his faith. The man couldn't have known what Jesus would do—whether

He'd help him get to the water on time, whether He'd leave him as he was, or something else altogether. Faith is a wonderful thing, because it allows us to receive whatever God will give us.

When Tony Campolo was in a church in Oregon, he prayed for a man who had cancer. In the middle of the week, he received a telephone call from the man's wife.

She said, "You prayed for my husband. He had cancer."

"Had?" *Whoa,* he thought, *it's happened!*

She said, "He died." Campolo felt terrible.

"Don't feel bad," the woman said. "When he came into church that Sunday, he was filled with anger. He knew he was going to be dead in a short period of time, and he hated God. He was fifty-eight years old, and he wanted to see his children and grandchildren grow up. He was angry that this all-powerful God didn't take away his sickness and heal him. He would lie in bed and curse God. The more his anger grew toward God, the more miserable he was to everybody around him. It was an awful thing to be in his presence. After you prayed for him, a peace came over him and a joy came into him. The last three days have been the best days of our lives. We've sung. We've laughed. We've read Scripture. We've prayed. Oh, they've been wonderful days. And I called to thank you for laying your hands on him and praying for healing." Then she said something incredibly profound: "He wasn't cured, but he was healed."[28]

---

[28]Tony Campolo, "Year of Jubilee," Preaching Today Audio, no. 212

Jesus wanted him to trust. The man had some legiti-mate excuses for being stuck in his *woundedness*—nobody was going to help him, and he was unable to help himself; but that didn't stop him from hoping. I kind of like the man's matter-of-fact tone. He was basically saying, "I'm ready and waiting."

"Come to me, all you who are weary and burdened, and I will give you rest. Take my yoke upon you and learn from me, for I am gentle and humble in heart, and you will find rest for your souls. For my yoke is easy and my burden is light."

—Matthew 11:28–30

Believing the Impossible

Then Jesus said to him, "Get up! Pick up your mat and walk." At once the man was cured; he picked up his mat and walked. The day on which this took place was a Sabbath, and so the Jews said to the man who had been healed, "It is the Sabbath; the law forbids you to carry your mat." But he replied, "The man who made me well said to me, 'Pick up your mat and walk.'" So they asked him, "Who is this fellow who told you to pick it up and walk?" The man who was healed had no idea who it was, for Jesus had slipped away into the crowd that was there. Later Jesus found him at the temple and said to him, "See, you are well again. Stop sinning or something worse may happen to you." The man went away and told the Jews that it was Jesus who had made him well.

—Matthew 11:8–15

Jesus is the healer of our diseases and the forgiver of our sins. Isn't it wonderful that God doesn't just make our bodies well, but our souls too? Imagine if we were all running around perfectly healthy without any knowledge about Jesus Christ? It would be cruel, to give us an illusion of wellness while we're heading for destruction—like a pilot coming out to serve everyone a hot meal while the plane heads straight for a cliff, or a doctor giving a cancer-ridden patient a clean bill of health. Jesus walks with us through the valley of the shadow of death and leads us to green pastures; it's not one without the other.

5

God Can Guide Me Even When The Lady On My GPS Gets Laryngitis

"It seems that millions of people accept Him as their Lord. That is, they gladly accept His offer of eternal salvation and confess their sins and profess Him to be their Savior in order to gain God's acceptance and escape the wrath of His judgment for our sins. But their spiritual development does not go much beyond the offer of salvation."

—George Barna, *Revolution*

In the aftermath of the death of John Kennedy, Jr. in 1999, amateur pilot Stephen Hedges wrote about the difficulty of flying a plane by instruments alone—a necessary skill if you want to fly at night or in fog. Without this skill, it is easy for a pilot to fall into an uncontrolled bank and crash.

During one instrument lesson, Hedges noted, "I flew the headings and turns as instructed, but even with ten hours of instrument flying in my logbook, I was amazed at how quickly the plane slid into a banking turn if I diverted my attention for just a few moments. The first time it happened, a pang of panic shot through me, a momentary fear that made it even more difficult to comprehend what the plane was doing." But when he heard his instructor next to him calmly say, "Watch your bank," Hedges quickly leveled the plane.[29]

Likewise, the Christian can easily get distracted when going through the foggy times of life. Seeking guidance is as easy—and as difficult—as looking to the Lord. He is always there, leading us and guiding us to safe places. It's our job to listen and to watch for His instructions.

[29]Mark Galli, "Guidance: Lesson from JFK Jr. Crash," Preaching Today.com

To man belong the plans of the heart, but from the Lord comes the reply of the tongue. All a man's ways seem innocent to him, but motives are weighed by the Lord. Commit to the Lord whatever you do, and your plans will succeed. The Lord works out everything for his own ends—even the wicked for a day of disaster.

—Proverbs 16:1-4

Guidance from God's Word

God could have written clear instructions to us about how to live, maybe periodically etching them across the sky in bold letters; but He chose to give us a book filled with poetry, stories, letters, prophecies, and revelations. This nebulous Book is our primary tool for understanding God's will.

That seems a bit scary at first, but the Bible is not so much an instruction book as it is a literary account of God's relationship with His people. God's intention never was to treat us like puppets or prisoners or pets. He will guide us, but not force us; He will lead us, but not take away our freedom.

So how do we get guidance from the Bible? First of all, we have to read it. Guidance doesn't come from putting our hands on its leather cover and gleaning wisdom by osmosis. Neither can we pick and choose random passages without understanding the whole message. Only by being familiar with the entire book—by studying individual passages and learning the overarching story—do we come to know the heart of God. Second, we hear from God through scripture by asking the Holy Spirit to open our spiritual eyes. The Word is living and active, and its truth comes upon us powerfully and unexpectedly from passages we thought we knew inside out, providing fresh insight to our specific situations.

If you haven't experienced this yet, press on. There is nothing more exciting than knowing God is speaking to you!

Don't miss out on the opportunity to pick up a Bible. In some countries, people have to pay with their lifeblood to get the Bible into the hands of believers; here, most of us have several copies sitting around in our homes. Don't let anything—not your lack of time, your lack of interest, your lack of perseverance—stop you from plucking the fruit of the Word that's dangling before you.

Trust in the LORD with all your heart and lean not on your own understanding; in all your ways acknowledge him, and he will make your paths straight.

—Proverbs 3:5-6

Guidance from Our Abilities and Gifts

Another way to discover the will of God is to pay attention to the passion He has put in your heart. He has blessed you with certain skills and interests—which fits into His master plan. When you live up to your potential, for His glory, you are following His will.

Sometimes it is *lack* of gifting that tells us what our next step should be. If you don't have a good singing voice, don't volunteer for the worship team—work with the kids instead. If you lose your temper with children, don't volunteer to teach Sunday school—bring a meal to someone in need instead. God expects you to use what you have well, not to excel at everything.

As the old joke goes: A golfer approached the first tee—a hazardous hole with a green surrounded by water—and debated if he should use his new golf ball. Deciding that the hole was too treacherous, he pulled out an old ball and placed it on the tee. Just then he heard a voice from above say loudly: "*Use the new ball!*" Frightened, he replaced the old ball with the new one and approached the tee. Now the voice from above instructed: "*Take a practice swing!*" With this, the golfer stepped backward and took a swing. The voice spoke one more time: "*Never mind. Use the old ball.*"

All kidding aside, seeking guidance based on your skills and abilities and passions is a tough one to negotiate, because you also have to be careful to not limit yourself to what you perceive to be within your skill set. If we were called to do only what we thought we could do, none of us would do the miraculous. I'm sure the apostles in the early church didn't wake up one morning and say to each other, "Hey, when we're preaching later today, let's all speak in a language we don't know. I think I'd be good at that." (See Acts 2.) That spiritual gifting was beyond their ability.

It was he who gave some to be apostles, some to be prophets, some to be evangelists, and some to be pastors and teachers, to prepare God's people for works of service, so that the body of Christ may be built up.

—Ephesians 4:11–12

Guidance from Life's Circumstances

One day Dwight Morrow and his wife, the parents of Anne Lindbergh, were in Rugby, England. After wandering through the streets they realized that they had lost their way. At this moment an incident occurred that entered into Morrow's philosophy and became a guiding principle in his life. He stopped a little Rugby lad of about twelve years. "Could you tell us the way to the station?" he asked. "Well," the boy answered, "You turn to the right there by the grocer's shop and then take the second street to the left. That will bring you to a place where four streets meet. And then, sir, you had better inquire again."[30]

We won't always have the full picture of God's plan for us, but He will give us enough guidance to know what we are supposed to do for now.

Events

Sometimes we tend to overthink—seeking God's will so earnestly that we don't see what is right before us. God may simply roll out His plan for you, and you just

[30]*Bits and Pieces*, December 1991, p. 14.

need to participate in the events that are unfolding. My rule of thumb: if your response to a situation is not contrary to biblical guidelines and there are no red flags, go for it. Don't wait for some magical sign from God.

It reminds me of the joke about a man clinging to his rooftop during a flood. He prays that God will send him deliverance, and pretty soon a man in a rowboat comes by. "No thanks," the man on the rooftop says, "I'm waiting on God to save me." Later a family paddles up to him on a raft, and finally a helicopter drops him a rope ladder, but the man gives the same reply. Finally, waves close over the rooftop and the man finds himself standing before God's throne. "I prayed to You, Lord!" he protests. "Why didn't You save me?"

"I sent you a rowboat, a raft, and a helicopter," the Lord replies. "What did you expect?"

I remember fondly the circumstances that let me to be a pastor. As a sixteen-year-old kid I was preaching at a Newark, Ohio youth crusade. A man there told me I should go home and quit preaching, but I fought off the attack of the enemy and prayed all night long before going to high school the next day and then driving thirty miles to Newark to preach the next evening. Good thing I prayed and felt strong enough to continue in the event that was unfolding, because it was that evening that the Westside Church met with me—almost all 17 regular attendees—and asked me to be their pastor.

Environment

God is sovereign. He placed you in your family, your country, your century, and your neighborhood for a reason. Where you now live and serve is no accident. God knows exactly what role He would have you play to bring about His kingdom. Now, if you choose to reject God's plan for you, or if you fail, or if you temporarily backslide—God's plan will not fail. He will raise up someone else to take your place or turn the situation around so that your mistake will work to His advantage. But wouldn't you rather get it right from the beginning?

And we know that in all things God works for the good of those who love him, who have been called according to his purpose.

—Romans 8:28

Accept your heritage. All of it, good or bad, shapes you into the person you are today—and that person is exactly the right person for the task God has prepared for you. You may have grown up in a bubble—in a safe home and family where you were taught from the Bible and where you saw the Christian example being lived out; you've been given invaluable resources that you can effectively share with others. Maybe you grew up in a home where Christian values were the last thing anyone cared about, and you saw the world up close and personal; let that experience fill you with compassion and grace. You may be wealthy or poor, black or white, male or female, educated or street smart, from a small town or a big city, from a powerful nation or forgotten country—God has given you exactly the right history and background for the task He has designed for you.

Don't be envious of the heritage of others or proud of the one that has been given to you; let it simply be what it is. Don't make excuses when God calls you to something based on your perceived resources; God knows what you can and can't do. Embrace who you are and where you are to serve the Lord.

Opportunities

It doesn't matter where you are or what skills you have or what events are unfolding before you if you don't have your eyes open to the opportunities God places before you. It's true that you need to be seeking God's wisdom through prayer and Bible reading, but then expect Him to lead you through opportunities.

Missionary Milton Cunningham provides a perfect example of this. He was flying on a plane from Atlanta to Dallas, and happened to have the middle of the three seats on one side of the aisle. To his right, sitting next to the window, was a young girl who obviously had Down's Syndrome.

"Mister," she said to Cunningham, "did you brush your teeth this morning?"

Cunningham, rather shocked at the question, squirmed around a bit and then said, "Well, yes, I brushed my teeth this morning."

The young girl said, "Good, 'cause that's what you're supposed to do." They she asked, "Mister, do you smoke?"

Again, Cunningham was a little uncomfortable, but he told her with a little chuckle that he didn't.

She said, "Good, 'cause smoking will make you die." Then she said, "Mister, do you love Jesus?"

Cunningham was really caught by the simplicity and the forthrightness of the little girl's questions. He smiled and said, "Well, yes, I do love Jesus."

The little girl with Down's Syndrome smiled and said, "Good, 'cause we're all supposed to love Jesus."

About that time, just before the plane was ready to leave, another man came and sat down on the aisle seat next to Cunningham and began to read a magazine. The little girl nudged Cunningham again and said, "Mister, ask him if he brushed his teeth this morning."

Cunningham was really uneasy with that one, and said that he didn't want to do it. But she kept nudging him and saying, "Ask him! Ask him!" So Cunningham turned to the man seated next to him and said, "Mister, I don't mean to bother you, but my friend here wants me to ask you if you brushed youth teeth this morning."

The man looked startled, of course. But when he looked past Cunningham and saw the young girl sitting there, he could tell her good intentions, so he took her question in stride and said with a smile, "Well, yes, I brushed my teeth this morning."

As the plane taxied onto the runway and began to take off, the young girl nudged Cunningham once more and said, "Ask him if he smokes." And so, good-naturedly, Cunningham did, and the man said that he didn't smoke.

As the plane was lifted into the air, the little girl nudged Cunningham once again and said, "Ask him if he loves Jesus."

Cunningham said, "I can't do that. That's too personal. I don't feel comfortable saying that to him."

But the girl insisted, "Ask him! Ask him!"

Cunningham turned to the fellow one more time and said, "Now she wants to know if you love Jesus."

The man could have responded like he had to the two previous questions—with a smile on his face and a little chuckle in his voice. And he almost did. But then the smile on his face disappeared, and his expression became serious. Finally he said to Cunningham, "You know, in all honesty, I can't say that I do. It's not that I don't want to; it's just that I don't know Him. I don't know how to know Him. I've wanted to be a person of faith all my life, but I haven't known how to do it. And now I've come to a time in my life when I really need that very much.[31]

Thank God for opportunities!

Guidance from Wise Counsel

Walter Knight told of an old Scottish woman who went from home to home across the countryside selling thread, buttons, and shoestrings. When she came to an unmarked crossroad, she would toss a stick into the air and go in the direction the stick pointed when it landed.

One day, however, she was seen tossing the stick up several times. "Why do you toss the stick more than once?" someone asked. "Because," replied the woman, "it keeps pointing to the left, and I want to take the road on the right." She then dutifully kept throwing the stick into the air until it pointed the way she wanted to go![32]

[31]Stan Toler, God Has Never Failed Me, 2010.
[32]Today in the World, May, 2010.

Sometimes we act as though we're seeking guidance from others, when in truth we already know exactly what we're going to do. We get guidance from people we know will agree with us—or at least won't disagree. We phrase our questions in such a way as to elicit the desired response. We hear from our advisors what we want to hear instead of what they're saying.

We're hurting ourselves when we ignore wise advice from others. They can give us a perspective that we don't have. They may have wisdom or knowledge or experience that we don't; they may be neutral about an issue that you can't help but be biased about. Listen to others; more than that, seek out their advice.

> Plans fail for lack of counsel, but with many advisers they succeed.
>
> —Proverbs 15:22

When I was asked to be a pastor of a certain church, I called Dr. Jerald Johnson, a general superintendent, saying that I didn't know what to do. "Here's what I think :" Dr. Johnson said, "don't do it!" It seemed bold at the time, but looking back I can see he was absolutely right.

For years, I believed that my career in ministry would always be as a pastor and I assumed that my entire work would be with local congregations. But, I got some great advice from two men I greatly respect, Dr. Talmadge Johnson and Dr. Carl Summer. They said, "Don't be so closed-minded!" So I opened my heart to the idea of serving beyond the local church. Sure enough, I was elected as a district superintendent later that year. That's when it got interesting. I had served as a district super-intendent for only eight hours when God guided people to elect me as a general superintendent—the same day I started my job as a district superintendent! I know now that it took my willingness to accept the first role in order for God to open up the next one.

Guidance from the Holy Spirit

One of the names given to the third member of the Trinity is *Counselor*. He is the one Counselor that you can always count on to be absolutely correct, unbiased, loving, and empowering. He wants to lead you and will speak directly to your heart.

> And I will ask the Father, and He will give you another Counselor to be with you forever.
>
> —John 14:16

My election as a general superintendent took place at the Church of the Nazarene General Assembly in Orlando, Florida, on July 2, 2009. The day progressed from serene to surreal to spectacular in a matter of hours. The assembly was progressing very well with great services marked by the Holy Spirit, a passionate stand for the holiness message, and great choices by the assembly for the new General Superintendents. I felt great about the three who were elected.

It was the last day of business and I was dressed in casual clothing when Dr. John Bowling chose to rescind his election. Balloting began immediately and in a brief time period, I realized that I was being seriously considered by the delegation for the role of General Superintendent. I stood in disbelief as the results of the final ballot announced and I was elected the thirty-ninth General Superintendent of the Church of the Nazarene. It was a God moment that I could not deny.

May God himself, the God of peace, sanctify you through and through. May your whole spirit, soul and body be kept blameless at the coming of our Lord Jesus Christ. The one who calls you is faithful and he will do it.

—1 Thessalonians 5:23-24

It's hard to explain how the Holy Spirit leads a person. It's a deeply personal and inexplicable thing, like having a food preference, or falling in love, or experiencing déjà vu, or dreaming. And it's also hard to explain how to seek the guidance of the Holy Spirit. The best I can do is to tell you to cry out to Him, tell Him what's on your heart, and listen and watch and feel for the response He will give you.

Crying out to the Holy Spirit is kind of like how a scuba diver figures out which way is up when he's in water so deep and dark that he's become disoriented. What a terrifying feeling—being underwater, unable to see your hands in front of your face, not knowing which way is up, panic engulfing you. So what do you do? Feel for bubbles. Bubbles always drift to the surface; so when you can't trust your feelings or judgment, you can always trust the bubbles to get you back to the top.

Seeking the will of God, by whichever of the means mentioned in this chapter, is an art, not a science. God is unchanging, but He's not predicable. He's a real Person, and our relationship with Him cannot be made into a formula.

Experiences of God cannot be planned or achieved. "They are spontaneous moments of grace, almost accidental," a rabbi said. His student asked, "If God-realization is just accidental, why do we work so hard doing all these spiritual practices?" "To be as accident-prone as possible," said the teacher.[33]

[33]Philip Yancey, *Prayer* (Zondervan, 2006).

6

God Can Empower Me Even When I Haven't Memorized The Names Of All The Kings In The Old Testament

Our sanctification does not depend upon changing our works, but in doing that for God's sake which we commonly do for our own. The time of business does not with me differ from the time of prayer.

—Brother Lawrence

We have been called to fulfill the mission of Christ in the world. That may sound intimidating, but be assured victorious Christian living is possible when we live in the power of the Spirit.

> You, dear children, are from God and have overcome them, because the one who is in you is greater than the one who is in the world.
>
> —1 John 4:4

Keep in mind that victorious living is possible *only* when we live in the power of the Spirit. It is God who sanctifies us to do good works; it is not the good works that make us holy.

I recently read nine holiness classics that have been out of print for years, just to remind myself of the thinking of great minds on this deep topic.

- Beliefs that Matter Most – W. T. Purkiser
- Entire Sanctification – C. B. Jernigan
- In His Likeness – John A. Knight
- Be Filled with the Spirit – W. S. Deal
- Holiness in Practical Living – L. T. Corlett
- Life in the Spirit – R. S. Taylor
- Holiness, The Heart of Christian Experience – J. B. Chapman

- Entire Sanctification Explained – C. W. Ruth
- ABC's of Holiness – D. Shelby Corlett

You might want to check out the books yourself, but I'll give you a teaser from some of them as we look at the basic principles of sanctification.

Filled with the Spirit

Sanctification is a big word with a big message. It has to do with being transformed—putting to death the sinful nature and allowing the Holy Spirit to lead us to righteous living. This transformation is not reserved for great Christian leaders or an elite group of chosen Christians. God offers this beautiful gift to each of us who call on the name of Jesus.

> When the heart has been made to long deeply for the Holy Spirit's fullness, we are then ready to receive the blessing.
>
> —William M. Greathouse

It's a powerful experience when the Holy Spirit begins working in you. You can sense the changes within yourself, and others take note as well. You are able to resist temptations that once consumed you. In fact, the very desires of your heart change and you become a new person. It's exciting to see yourself becoming the better person you've always wanted to be.

Be self-controlled and alert. Your enemy the devil prowls around like a roaring lion looking for someone to devour.

—1 Peter 5:8

Overcoming our Enemy is exciting and good, but the real power of sanctification is in how it causes us to reach out to others.

But you will receive power when the Holy Spirit comes on you; and you will be my witnesses in Jerusalem, and in all Judea and Samaria, and to the ends of the earth.

—Acts 1:8-11

Once we have tasted the goodness of God and experienced transformation, we are empowered to introduce others to Jesus so they too can have the life-altering experience of falling in love with Him. We can't save people by using excellent persuasive skills or even by showering them with love; it's only by the power of the Spirit that someone can have spiritual discernment.

The god of this age has blinded the minds of unbelievers, so that they cannot see the light of the gospel of the glory of Christ, who is the image of God.

—2 Corinthians 4:4

We simply give witness to what God has done for us, and the Spirit of God floods their souls, as He did ours.

In that way personal sanctification becomes corporate, shared, global—and the name of Christ is made known. Consider this report from *Trinity* magazine:

Bible college professor Yohanna Katanacho, who pastors a small church in Jerusalem, is subjected to much persecution. Israeli soldiers who patrol the city looking for potential terrorists impose spontaneous curfews on Palestinians and have the legal right to shoot at a Palestinian who does not respond quickly enough to their summons.

Yohanna tried and failed in his attempts to love his enemies. The Israeli soldiers' random daily checks for Palestinian identification cards—sometimes stopping them for hours—fed Yohanna's fear and anger. As he confessed his inability to God, Yohanna realized something significant. The radical love of Christ is not an emotion, but a decision. He decided to show love, however reluctantly, by sharing the gospel message with the soldiers on the street. With new resolution, Yohanna began to carry copies of a flyer with him, written in Hebrew and English, with a quotation from Isaiah 53 and the words "Real Love" printed across the top. Every time a soldier stopped him, he handed him his ID card and the flyer. Because the quote came from the Hebrew Scriptures, the soldier usually asked him about it before letting him go.

After several months, Yohanna realized his feelings toward the soldiers had changed. "I was surprised, you know?" he says. "It was a process, but I didn't pay attention to that process. My older feelings were not there anymore. I would pass in the same street, see the same soldiers as before, but now find myself praying, "Lord, let them stop me so that I can share with them the love of Christ."[34]

To Overcome Sin

D. Shelby Corlett says that holiness gives us a clear concept of the true, the right, the pure and the honest.[35]

According to a survey published by the Barna Group in 2006, most Americans don't consider themselves to be holy. Three out of four Americans believe it is possible for someone to become holy regardless of their past. However, only half of the adult population, said they knew someone they considered to be holy and only 21 percent considered themselves to be holy.

The views of born-again Christians were not much different from the national averages. Among believers, three-quarters said it is possible for a person to become holy regardless of his or her past. Slightly more than half of the group said they knew someone they would describe as holy. And roughly 29 percent said they themselves were holy, which is marginally more than the national norm.[36]

Do we consider ourselves so unholy because we're humble? Or do we really not live as we should? Maybe it's a bit of both. We can tend to be harsh judges of ourselves, but we can also tend to stray from what we know is right.

[34] "When Love Is Impossible," Trinity Magazine (Fall 2005)
[35] D. Shelby Corlett, Editor, Herald of Holiness, 1940.
[36] "The Concept of Holiness Baffles Most Americans," barna.org (February 20, 2006).

Perhaps it's time to quit feeling like failures, and simply do better.

> Do not get drunk on wine, which leads to debauchery. Instead, be filled with the Spirit.
> —Ephesians 5:18

We're so into authenticity these days (i.e., admitting that we're far from perfect) that we have started accepting our failures as normal. It's good to be humble and authentic. But, let's also be bold to claim the sanctification offered by the Holy Spirit so that we can overcome our sinful nature.

Removing our sinful nature could be compared to removing a tattoo—it's slow, painful, and costly. I doubt there is anyone getting a tattoo removed who doesn't think, "Why did I get this done in the first place." Take it a step further, though: imagine what is going through the thoughts of a person removing the tattoos that associate him with a gang. It's still slow, painful, and costly—but the hope of breaking free from a past that kept the person in bondage to despair and destruction would make up for it all. Even the process would be exhilarating—a stripping away of an identity no longer his into newfound freedom and hope.

Let's break free from our sins, put our past behind us, and begin a new life!

To Overcome Temptation

We don't need to give in to our temptations. It helps me to hear that. We really are able to resist. Just because a thought crosses my mind, I don't have to act on it. Just because you used to indulge in that sin, you don't have to anymore. L. T. Corlett says that holiness provides foundation for victory over temptation.[37]

No temptation has seized you except what is common to man. And God is faithful; he will not let you be tempted beyond what you can bear. But when you are tempted, he will also provide a way out so that you can stand up under it.
—2 Corinthians 10:13

Temptation is not sin; it is an opportunity to sin. It's a comfort to know that Jesus Himself was tempted (and yet was without sin). Sometimes, though, I wonder why temptation couldn't be removed altogether. Once we have been sanctified, shouldn't all our temptations disappear so we don't need to struggle anymore. Resisting temptation is hard work!

Consider Josie Caven, a little girl in England who was born profoundly deaf. She often felt isolated as a child because of her inability to hear, but that changed after she received a cochlear implant during the Christmas season. At the age of twelve, she heard clearly for the first time. The first sound she heard was the song "Jingle Bells" coming from the radio.

Was Josie's hearing restored? Yes—completely. Was she hearing well immediately? Not exactly. Her mother said, "She is having to learn what each new sound is and what it means. She will ask, 'Was that a door closing?'

---

[37]L. T. Corlett, Holiness in Practical Living, 1957.

and has realized for the first time that the light in her room hums when it is switched on. She even knows what her name sounds like now, because before she could not hear the soft *s* sound in the middle of the word. Seeing her face light up as she hears everything around her is all I could have wished for this Christmas."

Josie's hearing was restored, but that restoration introduced her to the daily adventure of learning to distinguish each new sound in the hearing world. It's the already and the not yet—a phrase that aptly describes the perspective of believers in Christ who have not yet experienced the fullness of redemption that will one day be realized in heaven.[38]

We are restored. We are sanctified and made holy—but we're not perfect. Not yet. Hang on, my friend. That day is coming!

To Overcome Problems

R. S. Taylor says that holiness is not an option. It is as essential for our spiritual life as food is for the physical life.[39]

Neglecting our spiritual life has serious consequences. If we don't exercise our newfound freedom in Christ, our spiritual muscles will atrophy. If we continue to be slaves to our old way of living, we'll become obese with sin.

Of course, negligence can cause things worse than lethargy to happen.

Consider the sad story of Anna Flores, thirty-six, who was walking with her toddler in downtown Chicago on a

[38]"Christmas Carols Music to the Ears of Deaf Girl," Yorkshireposttoday.com
[39]R. S. Taylor, Life in the Spirit, 1966.

warm autumn afternoon. She was killed when a window from the twenty-ninth floor of the CNA building fell and struck her in the head. What makes the story even worse is that CNA officials had known the window had been broken since June, but hadn't made the time to fix it.

If you are aware of a spiritual problem in your life, don't neglect it! Address the issue before it causes death for all eternity. If the Holy Spirit has opened your eyes to a problem, that means He will help you find the solution. Once you experience the power of the Holy Spirit, you simply can't continue living the way you always have. That would be like eating a cookie after someone told you the "chocolate chips" were really mouse droppings.

You know better now. You can *see*.

"Don't be afraid," the prophet answered. "Those who are with us are more than those who are with them." And Elisha prayed, "O Lord, open his eyes so he may see." Then the Lord opened the servant's eyes, and he looked and saw the hills full of horses and chariots of fire all around Elisha.

—2 Kings 6:16–17

When the Holy Spirit opens our eyes to see that the Lord is empowering us to enter His beautiful kingdom, our problems don't seem so bad and our choices become clear. When we let our problems consume us, we become like the spouse attending a counseling session only for the sake of appearances. He or she doesn't really believe the marriage will work—or doesn't really want it to—but attends the counseling session either to

God Can Empower Me Even When I Haven't Memorized The Names Of All The Kings In The Old Testament prove it's hopeless or to make it look like the separation is the other person's fault. If this person had spiritual eyes, he or she would look for solutions, make changes, and believe better things are yet to come.

The Holy Spirit knows the problems we face, and is not overwhelmed by them. He will open our eyes to see the resources we have to overcome them.

To overcome doubt

It's probably true that every Christian has gone through a time of doubting. I suppose doubt may be a pathway to true faith—almost like we have to see the other side before we can fully embrace the Truth.

But doubting is not a fun process. The power of doubt is strong.

> They are from the world and therefore speak from the viewpoint of the world, and the world listens to them.
>
> —1 John 4:5

Some people doubt whether God really cares, whether Jesus is really the Son of God, whether He really rose from the dead, whether the Holy Spirit is really at work in the world. Some people begin doubting their own experiences. They may have had an encounter with the Holy Spirit that was profound and life changing—only to wonder later if the experience was a figment of their imagination.

That's why the Holy Spirit continues to live in us, to move in our lives, to give us new experiences. He's alive and active. Our task is to stay open to Him, watching for Him. Alister McGrath paints a lovely picture of remembering.

My aunt had died, having lived to be eighty or so. She had never married. While clearing out her possessions, we came across a battered photograph of a young man whom my aunt had loved. The relationship had ended tragically. She never loved anyone else and kept for the remainder of her life a photograph of the man she had loved.

Why? As she aged, she knew that she would have difficulty believing that, at one point in her life, someone had once cared for her and regarded her as his everything. It could all have seemed a dream, an illusion, something she had invented in her old age to console her in her declining years—except for the photo. The photo reminded her that she really had loved someone once and was loved in return. It was her sole link to a world in which she had been valued.

Communion bread and wine, like that photograph, reassure us that something that seems too good to be true—something that we might even be suspected of having invented—really did happen.[40]

One difference between remembering true love and remembering when the Holy Spirit moved in your heart

[40]Alister McGrath, Doubting: Growing through the Uncertainties of Faith (InterVarsity, 2006).

is that the Holy Spirit is still there. At any time you can talk to Him, cry to Him, seek Him—and He is there to guide, comfort, and assure.

The Spirit at Works within Us

God is a Person. He is Someone we can have a relationship with—not someone who forces religious practices on us.

As God has said: "I will live with them and walk among them, and I will be their God, and they will be my people."

—2 Corinthians 6:16

He sent his Son to die for our sins so that we can be made holy and come into His presence—and He sent His Spirit to remain with us until Jesus comes again. What a wonderful God!

And this is his command: to believe in the name of his Son, Jesus Christ, and to love one another as he commanded us. Those who obey his commands live in him, and he in them. And this is how we know that he lives in us: We know it by the Spirit he gave us.

—1 John 3:23-24

Residing
You most likely have a home. This is where you belong; it's the hub of all your activities. The Holy Spirit

makes His home in the hearts of those who love God. This is where He belongs and the base from which He does His activities in the world.

To make your heart the home of the Holy Spirit, you must know and love the Lord. You must welcome the Spirit into your life. C. W. Ruth says there must be a complete yielding an unconditional surrender to God.[41]

I think many Christians want this on one level—we may even say the words of invitation to the Holy Spirit, but some of us aren't quite ready to surrender. We don't really want to give up control of our lives, and we're not convinced that God's will is better than our own.

It's kind of like wearing a seatbelt. Of course, we understand that wearing one provides protection for us, and we usually intend to pull the thing over our shoulder. But we don't always get around to it. We may be in a hurry, or we may figure we probably won't get in an accident anyway, so why bother.

Imagine, however, going to visit a loved one in the hospital after a serious car accident—where she was thrown through the front windshield because she was not wearing a seatbelt. She may be on life support, and not able to communicate with you. Perhaps she has hundreds of stitches on her face and numerous broken bones. After an incident like that, you suddenly think of your seatbelt in a whole new way. You can't get into the car without thinking of your loved one, and you deliberately pull your seatbelt on before you even start the car. The importance of wearing a seatbelt has gone from head knowledge to heart

---

[41]C. W. Ruth, Entire Sanctification Explained, 1939.

knowledge, and you'll never revert back to the way it was before.

Put on your seatbelt! What I mean is: Accept the Holy Spirit into your heart. Don't wait until it's too late. He offers you so much, and you only have to accept. Not having the Holy Spirit when you know the Lord is like trying to call 9-1-1 on a cell phone with a dead battery. It's like setting up a huge display of fireworks without bringing any matches or lighters. It's like eating nothing but junk food before a big race.

It's even worse than that. Denying the power of the Spirit in your life by not allowing your heart to be His home is godlessness. Scripture says, "There will be terrible times the last days. People will be ... having a form of godliness but denying its power. Have nothing to do with them" (2 Timothy 3:1, 5).

It's a beautiful mystery—having the Almighty God make residence in our hearts. The only way to understand it is to experience it.

> To them God has chosen to make known among the Gentiles the glorious riches of this mystery, which is Christ in you, the hope of glory.
>
> —Colossians 1:27

Abiding

I love the connotation associated with the word *abide*. It's so warm and comforting. It's secure and stable. It has nothing to do with the disconnected, fast-paced world in which we live; it has everything to do with resting, nestling, connecting.

I also like the image of the branches being connected to the vine that Jesus uses to teach what it means to abide.

I am the true vine, and my father is the gardener. He cuts off every branch that bears no fruit, while every branch that does bear fruit he prunes so that it will be even more fruitful.... Remain in me, and I will remain in you.

—John 15:1–4

When the Counselor comes, whom I will send to you from the Father, the Spirit of truth who goes out from the Father, he will testify about me.

—John 15:26

We abide in Christ and He abides in us, through the Holy Spirit. Living this way, day after day, is comforting and powerful at once. Of course, abiding, by its very nature, is not exciting—it's consistent. And, just as you may not hear white noise until it's turned off, you may not always be aware of the radical presence of God in you. We can tune out the Spirit when He becomes so familiar to us, just as we can do with so many other things.

Christo and Jeanne-Claude, environmentalist artists, have made it their task to open people's eyes to the beauty all around them. Aware that people were taking the beauty of nature for granted, this couple found a way to make people pay attention. They study magnificent natural views, and craft a way to draw attention to it for a short period of time. "In doing so, we see and perceive the whole environment with new eyes and a new consciousness," Christo and Jeanne-Claude say on their website. For instance, they hung 142,000 square feet of orange nylon fabric between the mountains on either side of Rifle Gap in Colorado in the early 1970s. Ten years later they surrounded two islands off the Florida coast in bright pink fabric. Later they "wrapped" the German Reichstag and the Pont Neuf in France. Each project typically requires years of logistical planning and negotiations with local governments. The artwork demands sophisticated feats of engineering and hundreds of crew members, not to mention lots of money.

Their work is not appreciated by everyone. Some consider it ugly or distracting—but everyone must admit they are usually completely unprepared for what they are about to experience.[42]

We have to be intentional about keeping ourselves aware of the Holy Spirit abiding in us—by joining in corporate worship, through prayer, by living out His calling in our lives.

Presiding

You know the sound of the hammer hitting the bench in a courtroom? It has authority, doesn't it? That heavy, imposing thump makes us realize the judge is presiding over that room. For obvious reasons, the gavel is used at political conventions to signal the start of the convention—including at the Republican Convention in July 2000. However, the audio engineer at that event discovered that the noise the gavel actually made was too quiet to fill the hall, so he recorded an "ideal gavel sound" that was played over the loudspeakers when the

---

[42] "Central Park's Bright New Clothes," npr.org (February 10, 2005).

moderator struck the desk with the stand-in gavel.

I find that so interesting! On it's own that little gavel was powerless, unnoticeable—but with some help it launched an important national meeting. Doesn't that remind you of life as a Christian? On our own, we are pitifully small. But when the Spirit amplifies our voice, we can change the world.

Listen, the Holy Spirit doesn't just hang out within in us—He presides. He is the one who speaks into our lives and through our lives. On our own, we're just not powerful enough.

D. Shelby Corlett says, "Throughout Scripture, the word *sanctify* and it's related word *holy* conveys one primary idea, namely full devotedness to God." When we are fully open to Him, allowing Him to preside over our life, we experience true sanctification.

He will bring glory to me by taking from what is mine and making it known to you.
—John 16:14

When we are truly sanctified we long to give glory to Christ. It's not an obligation, but an exciting opportunity. We get the same kind of joy a woman named Marilyn Adamson had on a flight from Chicago to Lincoln, Nebraska.

I sat next to a Saudi Arabian guy, Ali, who was on his way to start college in Lincoln. As soon as I heard that he'd never been in the United States before and was from the Middle East, I felt Jesus tugging at my heart.

After a little chitchat about his feelings about being so far from home and asking what he knew about American culture or life in Nebraska, I told him I was a follower of Jesus.

I asked Ali about his spiritual background. I told him that he'd probably meet a number of people in Nebraska who are Christians, and said it'd probably be helpful to understand a little of where they're coming from. I pulled out the *Four Spiritual Laws* and read through each point with him.

We talked a little bit more, and then I went back to reading my book. He opened the booklet and read it cover to cover. I was so excited. I prayed for him as he was reading it, thankful to have been reminded this morning that God is the one who works, convicting people of their need for him. After Ali finished reading, I asked him what he thought, and he said it was very interesting.

As the plane landed I told him I'd pray for him, then was convicted that I should do it right then. I asked if I could pray for him, and he immediately said yes. At the baggage claim I went over and met his cousin and invited them both to an American cultural event—Christmas Eve Service at our church! We'll see! This is why I love being a Christian—it's heart-pounding scary at times and exhilarating when I see someone I know Jesus wants to come to him, and I have the choice to step out in faith or stay in security.[43]

[43]Craig Brian Larson and Phyllis Ten Elshof, eds., *1001 Sermon Illustrations That Connect* (Grand Rapids, Mich.: Zondervan, 2008), 62–63.

God Can Do Anything But Fail

God Can Use Me Even When I Can't Read The Fine Print Without A Telescope

> *Give me one hundred people who love nothing but God, hate nothing but evil, and know nothing but Jesus Christ, and I will change the world.*
>
> —John Wesley

I was honored to serve as pastor to the missionary famous Hawk family in southern Ohio. They sold their wonderful farm, and in 1959, Don Hawk took his wife and five children to Miami and boarded a boat for Honduras. Although he never graduated from college and didn't speak Spanish, He launched the El Sembrador Farm School. Today his children serve as missionaries and now his grandchildren also serve as missionaries.

The Hawks are no different than you and me. They are children of God empowered by the Holy Spirit to do extraordinary things.

Discovering God's Call

Being Alone with God

Many of us are afraid to be alone with ourselves. We turn on the television or radio to distract ourselves from our interior thoughts. We keep ourselves so busy throughout the day that we collapse into bed without taking a moment to contemplate deeper things.

How much scarier is it to be alone with God? God sees into our soul and knows every hidden thing. Almost every time a person in the Bible encounters the Lord, he falls flat on his face—terrified and profoundly aware of his own brokenness. No wonder we're afraid.

And yet, being alone with God is exactly what we need to understand what He expects from us.

Moses was a man who had experienced the majestic courts of Pharaoh and the hand of God blessing a nation. However, he was a person who was plagued with self-doubt and the fear of rejection. It wasn't until he was alone with God that Moses discovered a holy peace.

Now Moses was tending the flock of Jethro his fatherinlaw, the priest of Midian, and he led the flock to the far side of the desert and came to Horeb, the mountain of God. There the angel of the Lord appeared to him in flames of fire from within a bush. Moses saw that though the bush was on fire it did not burn up. So Moses thought, "I will go over and see this strange sight—why the bush does not burn up."

When the LORD saw that he had gone over to look, God called to him from within the bush, "Moses! Moses!"

And Moses said, "Here I am."

"Do not come any closer," God said. "Take off your sandals, for the place where you are standing is holy ground." Then he said, "I am the God of your father, the God of Abraham, the God of Isaac and the God of Jacob." At this, Moses hid his face, because he was afraid to look at God.

The LORD said, "I have indeed seen the misery of my people in Egypt. I have heard them crying out because of their slave drivers, and I am concerned

about their suffering. So I have come down to rescue them from the hand of the Egyptians and to
bring them up out of that land into a good and
spacious land, a land flowing with milk and
honey—the home of the Canaanites, Hittites,
Amorites, Perizzites, Hivites and Jebusites. And
now the cry of the Israelites has reached me, and I
have seen the way the Egyptians are oppressing
them."

—Exodus 3:1-9

When we enter that holy communion with the Lord
we discover a place where we have never before been.

- A place of obedience.
- A place of devotion.
- A place of revelation.
- A place of maturation.

Just as Moses entered into a new relationship with
God after all the distractions were removed from him so
he could be alone with God, so we too will be born
again.

Overcoming Excuses

When we meet God in a secret place, it's not like
everything will suddenly be made easy. Actually, it's
more likely that such a connection with God means He is
about to call you to something impossible. It means you

know you are ready to step out of your comfort zone and trust Him to accomplish something through you.

> "So now, go. I am sending you to Pharaoh to bring my people the Israelites out of Egypt."
>
> —Exodus 3:10

And, like Moses, you might resist.

> But Moses said to God, "Who am I, that I should go to Pharaoh and bring the Israelites out of Egypt?" And God said, "I will be with you. And this will be the sign to you that it is I who have sent you: When you have brought the people out of Egypt, you will worship God on this mountain."
>
> —Exodus 3:11–12

Can you imagine? I can't decide whether I would have been excited or horrified to be given such a huge task. I suppose I don't need to wonder; how I respond to God's call to me now is exactly what I would have done in Moses' place.

As for Moses, his self-esteem was challenged through the call of God, and he made various excuses in an attempt to get out of it—excuses I can relate to a little too well.

Excuse No. 1: Ignorance

Sometimes we feel like we just don't know enough.

> Moses said to God, "Suppose I go to the Israelites and say to them, 'The God of your fathers has sent

me to you,' and they ask me, 'What is his name?'
Then what shall I tell them?"

—Exodus 3:13

It's not that Moses was just coming up with random excuses—he really didn't know what he should say. Remember, the Bible didn't yet exist, and he didn't have years of Sunday School class behind him to help him rattle off the names of God. I think Moses truly felt unprepared for the task God called him to accomplish.

I know how that feels. I used to listen to a radio preacher when I was a kid in West Virginia and often heard him say, "God uses ignorant and unlearned people and I pray that He will make me more ignorant every day." While I wouldn't recommend praying that prayer, I believe God has and will use ignorant people to do His work. Just look at His disciples.

I pray every day that God will make me a godly disciple and that he will give me His answers.

God said to Moses, "I am who I am. This is what you are to say to the Israelites: 'I AM has sent me to you.'" God also said to Moses, "Say to the Israelites, 'The LORD, the God of your fathers—the God of Abraham, the God of Isaac and the God of Jacob—has sent me to you.' This is my name forever, the name by which I am to be remembered from generation to generation."

—Exodus 3:14–15

Excuse No. 2: Authority

Sometimes we don't want to do what God asks us to because we're pretty sure no one will listen to us.

> Moses answered, "What if they do not believe me or listen to me and say, 'The LORD did not appear to you'?"
>
> —Exodus 4:1

It's interesting to me that Moses, who was raised in Pharaoh's house, felt like he had no authority. I could see why a kid who works at McDonalds might think his words would be disregarded, but Moses was not young and he was not unknown—he was a prince! Don't people listen to people of royalty?

Listen, when you are telling countercultural things—like, that God spoke to you from a burning bush—people probably won't take you seriously. No matter how important you are. What you have to remember, though, is that you are not speaking out of your own authority; you are speaking out of God's.

> When Jesus had finished saying these things, the crowds were amazed at his teaching, because he taught as one who had authority, and not as their teachers of the law.
>
> —Matthew 7:28–29

Excuse No. 3: Inadequacy

Sometimes we don't want to do what God asks because we know we're not able to do it. We don't have the skills or the resources or the charisma. Or it's just plain impossible.

> Moses said to the LORD, "O LORD, I have never been eloquent, neither in the past nor since you have spoken to your servant. I am slow of speech and tongue."
>
> —Exodus 4:10

Moses acts as if God didn't know he was awkward with words, as if God would say, "Really? Well, I better go find someone who is more articulate." God is the one who made us, who gave us gifts and skills and resources and personality. He knows our strengths and our inadequacies—He designed us exactly for the time and place and circumstances in which we find ourselves. He placed us here because we are uniquely able to do His will for the sake of the Kingdom.

> The LORD said to him, "Who gave man his mouth? Who makes him deaf or mute? Who gives him sight or makes him blind? Is it not I, the LORD? Now go; I will help you speak and will teach you what to say."
>
> —Exodus 4:11–12

Excuse No. 4: Self-doubt

Sometimes we have no excuse; we just don't feel comfortable with the job. No amount of persuasion or logic will talk us into doing the right thing, the thing that God calls us to, because its really a matter of the heart.

But Moses said, "O Lord, please send someone else to do it. Then the Lord's anger burned against Moses."

—Exodus 4:13–14

Moses was more afraid of people not believing him than he was of angering the Lord. Before we judge him too harshly, let's think about our own lives. Do we ever hold back from telling people about Jesus because we know we'll look silly? Do we ever neglect the poor among us because we don't want to upset our spouse by giving away too much money? Do we ever go along with whatever everyone else is doing even when it is contrary to our beliefs just to avoid making waves?

Consider Connie Rehm, a librarian in Savannah, Missouri, who wouldn't work on Sunday so she could have a day of rest and attend church. As a result, she was terminated by the library. Connie decided to file a lawsuit, claiming religious discrimination, and the library immediately offered a financial settlement. But Connie didn't want the money; she wanted to keep her job! Three years after her initial termination in 2003, a Missouri jury ordered the library to reinstate Connie Rehm to her job. It also awarded her $53,712 in damages as compensation for lost wages. Rehm has an interesting thought about the incident: "A middle-American, mild-mannered, small-town library person—I attribute to the Lord a great sense of humor for having picked me for this test."[44]

God know exactly what He's doing when He picks us for a job—even if we don't.

[44]Dana Fields, "Woman Wins Religious Discrimination Case," *Houston Chronicle* (November 16, 2006).

Acting Boldly

Moses came up with all kinds of excuses, but when all was said and done, he obeyed.

So Moses took his wife and sons, put them on a donkey and started back to Egypt. And he took the staff of God in his hand.

—Exodus 4:20

He finally aligned with the will of God. He realized God would use the ordinary to do the extraordinary. And his dedication and willingness moved the heart of God.

We really can act boldly when God calls us to something. Think of Franklin D. Roosevelt who, taking office in 1933, confronted a country in crisis. Four in ten working-age Americans were jobless. Banks were collapsing. There were long lines outside tellers' windows as people rushed to withdraw their savings.

On March 4, Roosevelt gave his now famous inaugural address, promising that "the only thing we have to fear is fear itself." Within days he had secured legislation guaranteeing the banks, and on March 12 he took to the radio for the first of his fireside chats. "When the people find out that they can get their money and that they can get it when they want it the phantom of fear will soon be laid," he soothed an anxious nation. "I can assure you, it is safer to keep your money in a re-opened bank than under your mattress."

When banks re-opened the next morning, the lines were gone, as Robert A. Caro recounted in the first volume of his biography of Lyndon Johnson, "The Path to Power." People put money back in, so much that on the first day after the chat, deposits outweighed withdrawals by $10 million.

It was the legislation, but mostly, Mr. Caro writes: "Their confidence was restored by his confidence ..."[45]

Satan seeks to destroy, wreck, oppress and defeat every child of God. His method is to cause you to be doubtful and to fear the circumstances. He wants you to focus on your problems rather than your position in Christ. One of my favorite passages of Scripture is found in Isaiah 54:17, "No weapon forged against you will prevail, and you will refute every tongue that accuses you. This is the heritage of the servants of the LORD, and this is their vindication from me," declares the LORD." I am reminded of David going to battle with Goliath. "You come against me with sword and spear and javelin, but I come against you in the name of the LORD Almighty ... for the battle is the Lord's" (1 Samuel 17:45, 47). We gather together to gain strength and courage to go out tomorrow and do battle. We need a fresh baptism of "Believe It" faith, rather than "See it" faith. We must believe it in order to see it.

Don't let fear and doubt and insecurity stop you from experiencing the power of God in your life. God has a plan, and you are a part of it. Don't miss out!

---

[45]New York Times, Feb. 23, 2008, Kate Zernike, author.

Responding to God's Calling

The apostle Paul clearly lays out what it means to be called into the service of God. His testimony of God's call upon his life should be an encouragement to all believers. All God's children have a calling.

> But when God, who set me apart from birth and called me by his grace, was pleased.
> —Galatians 1:15

Reacting to the Call

He received the word. Paul did not create the message that he preached. He passed on only what he had been given. God called him to preach, and God gave him the message. We cannot give to others something we do not possess ourselves.

> I want you to know, brothers, that the gospel I preached is not something that man made up. I did not receive it from any man, nor was I taught it; rather, I received it by revelation from Jesus Christ.
> —Galatians 1:11–12

He repented of his failures. Nobody was a worse sinner than Paul was—truly! He called himself the chief among sinners; he was thoroughly familiar with his shortcomings. Yet he was fit for ministry after he had been pardoned for his past. No one who has been transformed by the grace of God is unfit for ministry. God can call any of us!

For you have heard of my previous way of life in Judaism, how intensely I persecuted the church of God and tried to destroy it. I was advancing in Judaism beyond many Jews of my own age and was extremely zealous for the traditions of my fathers.

—Galatians 1:13–14

He recognized its importance. The call to minister in the name of Jesus is a high calling indeed. We must respect the value of the call that God places upon our lives. It calls for our best energy, are highest aspirations, and our diligent effort in preparing ourselves to serve.

But when God, who set me apart from birth and called me by his grace, was pleased to reveal his Son in me so that I might preach him among the Gentiles, I did not consult any man, nor did I go up to Jerusalem to see those who were apostles before I was, but I went immediately into Arabia and later returned to Damascus.

—Galatians 1:15–17

He related to the family. Paul knew better than to undertake ministry on his own. He realized that he needed the support, affirmation, and recommendation of the wider Christian community. The same is true for you and me. We need the approval of our brothers and sisters in Christ if we are to be effective for the Lord.

Then after three years, I went up to Jerusalem to get acquainted with Peter and stayed with him fifteen days. I saw none of the other apostles—only James, the Lord's brother. I assure you before God that what I am writing you is no lie. Later I went to Syria and Cilicia. I was personally unknown to the churches of Judea that are in Christ. They only heard the report: "The man who formerly persecuted us is now preaching the faith he once tried to destroy." And they praised God because of me.

—Galatians 1:18-24

Those are the steps Paul took. Our circumstances are different, and none of us will respond in the exact same way to God. But its important to be intentional about responding. How are you reacting the call of God on your life? Knowing that you are His child—redeemed and prepared for the work of His kingdom—what are the steps you have taken or are taking?

Identifying with the Call

We experience saving grace. Our call from God begins with the call to salvation. No one can be appointed to serve who has not first met the Master. We cannot be His witnesses if we have not seen Him for ourselves.

And we have seen and testify that the Father has sent his Son to be the Savior of the world.

—1 John 4:14

We experience sanctifying grace. Jesus wants to do more than merely save us from hell. That would be salvation enough, but there is more! He wants to cleanse our hearts from sin so that we can be fully devoted to Him. Our call to service is furthered by this experience of holiness. When we have been set apart and cleansed, we are ready to be used by God.

> May God himself, the God of peace, sanctify you through and through. May your whole spirit, soul and body be kept blameless at the coming of our Lord Jesus Christ. The one who calls you is faithful and he will do it.
>
> —1 Thessalonians 5:23–24

We experience sustaining grace. The work of God in our lives is not a once-for-life event. He continues this saving work in us, sustaining us each day. Through the Holy Spirit, God gives us the strength to resist temptation, and He makes us adequate for the larger-than-life-sized challenges of ministry. We need His sustaining grace every day.

> You will seek me and find me when you seek me with all your heart.
>
> —Jeremiah 29:13

We experience sending grace. "How will I know where to go? How will I know what to say? How will I know what to do?" These are legitimate questions for the servant of Jesus. Fortunately, there is a simple answer. God will make these things known to us through His Holy Spirit.

Again Jesus said, "Peace be with you! As the Father has sent me, I am sending you."

—John 20:21

Are you aware that if you are saved, you are also called? Are you ready to accept not just His grace and love and forgiveness and acceptance, but also His calling? Will you raise your hand and say, "Send me" when He is looking for someone to do His will?

Understanding the Call

I often think that if I just knew what God wanted from me, I would do it. The thing is, I do know what God wants from me—it's just not always that grandiose adventure that I have in mind. More often it's just living in a way that is pleasing to Him.

All believers are gifted by God. Ministry is not just for the few, the proud, the ordained clergy! Every believer is gifted by God to serve others, regardless of whether he or she is called to vocational ministry. Are you born again? Then you can be sure God has a ministry picked out just for you!

There are different kinds of gifts, but the same Spirit. There are different kinds of service, but the same Lord. There are different kinds of working, but the same God works all of them in all men. Now to each one the manifestation of the Spirit is given for the common good. To one there is given through the Spirit the message of wisdom, to another the message of knowledge by means of the same Spirit, to another faith by the same Spirit, to another gifts of healing by that one Spirit, to another miraculous powers, to another prophecy, to another distinguishing between spirits, to another speaking in different kinds of tongues, and to still another the interpretation of tongues. All these are the work of one and the same Spirit, and he gives them to each one, just as he determines.

—1 Corinthians 12:4-11

All believers are gifted by God.. Quiet! Do you hear that? It is the still, small voice of God, tugging at your heart. Maybe He is arousing your compassion for the homeless. Perhaps He is giving you a burden for children or young people. Maybe He is calling you to preach! Whatever the call may be, you can be sure it is God's personal invitation for you to join Him in the great work of transforming the world.

We have different gifts, according to the grace given us. If a man's gift is prophesying, let him use it in proportion to his faith. If it is serving, let him serve; if it is teaching, let him teach; if it is encouraging, let him encourage; if it is contributing to the needs of others, let him give generously; if it is leadership, let him govern diligently; if it is showing mercy, let him do it cheerfully.

—Romans 12:6-8

All believers are used by God. Most people wonder what they could do that will make a difference in the world—or at least in the life of one other person. If I try to serve, will it matter? What if I fail? Is there anything I can do that will make a difference? Yes, there is! God uses all of us in different ways. You will be effective, right where you are. God will make it so.

> Each one should use whatever gift he has received to serve others, faithfully administering God's grace in its various forms. If anyone speaks, he should do it as one speaking the very words of God. If anyone serves, he should do it with the strength God provides, so that in all things God may be praised through Jesus Christ. To him be the glory and the power for ever and ever. Amen. Dear friends, do not be surprised at the painful trial you are suffering, as though something strange were happening to you.
>
> —1 Peter 4:10-12

Ask God to make it clear to you how you might serve Him. Be diligent in pursuing an answer, and be open to what He may have for you.

Obeying the Call

Paul, who was once a passionate persecutor of the followers of Jesus, responded to the call of God after his profound experience with Jesus. He responded immediately, and he responded consistently for the rest of his life.

> Nor did I go up to Jerusalem to see those who were apostles before I was, but I went immediately into

Arabia and later returned to Damascus. Then after three years, I went up to Jerusalem to get acquainted with Peter and stayed with him fifteen days. I saw none of the other apostles—only James, the Lord's brother. I assure you before God that what I am writing you is no lie. Later I went to Syria and Cilicia. I was personally unknown to the churches of Judea that are in Christ. They only heard the report: "The man who formerly persecuted us is now preaching the faith he once tried to destroy." And they praised God because of me.

—1 Peter 17–24

We must surrender to the will of God. Your heart is a battleground. It is the field of combat where your ego is in conflict with your Maker. Each of us naturally desires to have our own way in life. We want what we think is best for ourselves. To answer God's call on your life, you must surrender your own selfish desires and submit to His will. You can serve God, or you can serve yourself. You cannot do both at the same time.

Do not offer the parts of your body to sin, as instruments of wickedness, but rather offer yourselves to God, as those who have been brought from death to life; and offer the parts of your body to him as instruments of righteousness.

—Romans 6:13

We must study the Word of God. You and I may want to help people recover from illness, but wishing for it is not enough. If we want to enter the medical profession, we must study medical science. Likewise, if you want to help others grow in their relationship with God, you must study the Word of God. We do not teach our own ideas or any passing fad. We teach the Word, and we must be people of the Word in order to do so.

> I pray that out of his glorious riches he may strengthen you with power through his Spirit in your inner being.
> —Ephesians 3:16

We must seek the fullness of God's Spirit. It is good to know that we are not left alone in this task of ministry. God has not only called us and gifted us, but He guides us as well. Through His Holy Spirit, He gives us wisdom, strength, energy, and even the words to speak. When we seek His Spirit, we find the resources that we need. He is our Counselor.

> But the Counselor, the Holy Spirit, whom the Father will send in my name, will teach you all things and will remind you of everything I have said to you.
> —John 14:26

The amazing thing about being faithful to live righteously and using your gifts in love is that the grandiose adventure happens. You may think your daily life is mundane, but when you look back, you see how powerful the journey has been.

Exploring God's Call

Our Father in heaven is wonderful. He loves us so much, and gets pleasure out of blessing us. We are His children, after all.

Every good and perfect gift is from above, coming down from the Father of the heavenly lights, who does not change like shifting shadows.

—James 1:17

A Giver of Good Gifts

Personal Gifts. God gives gifts that we need, things that we are compelled to use, things that we could not live without. These gifts are often specific to you and your circumstances.

While kayaking in southern England off the Isle of Wight, Mark Ashton-Smith, a lecturer at Cambridge University, capsized in treacherous waters. Clinging to his craft and reaching for his cell phone, Ashton-Smith, thirty-three, called his dad. It didn't matter that his father, Alan Pimm-Smith, was training British troops in Dubai 3,500 miles away. Without delay, the father relayed his son's Mayday to the Coast Guard nearest to his son. Within twelve minutes, a helicopter retrieved the grateful Ashton-Smith. Like this kayaker, when we are in peril, our first impulse should be to call our Father—the one we trust to help us. He will give us what we need.[46]

[46] "Capsized Man Phones for Help 3,500 Miles Away," Reuters News Agency (September 11, 2001).

Powerful Gifts. God gives gifts that are practical, within our ability to use, that can be used to maximum potential. Don't be scared of the gifts He gives you. If He gives it to you, it fits. His gifts are not like a chain saw in the crib of an infant, or a Blackberry in a country with no cell service, or an air conditioner in the arctic. His gifts are potent—like a violin in the hand of a master musician. What He gives you, you can use.

Purposeful Gifts. God gives gifts that are helpful to the body of Christ. Every believer has at least one spiritual gift. All believers should employ theirs in the service of the Lord. Using our gifts for ourselves rather than others is like preparing a Christmas dinner for one person. The joy is in sharing, not hoarding. Hoarding, in fact, leads to destruction. If we keep our gifts to ourselves, they become rancid—just as the leftover food would after a feast for one.

> If you, then, though you are evil, know how to give good gifts to your children, how much more will your Father in heaven give good gifts to those who ask him!
>
> —Matthew 7:11

Enduring Gifts

We are blessed to be a blessing, but that doesn't mean we can't enjoy the blessing. Don't think for a moment that God is giving you something *only* so that you can use that gift for His sake. Part of the reason He wants us to use our gifts is because He knows that blessing others is itself a blessing. Your joy gives Him joy.

My friend has a cat that she simply adores. "That silly thing is the only creature in the world that doesn't seem to have a care in the world," she says. "And I want to keep it that way." She delights in knowing she is providing a good life for her pet. I admit I expected the cat to be overweight and spoiled, but he wasn't. He enjoyed hunting outside on the farm, and would sometimes be gone for days. He ate only the food he caught, supplemented by dry food packed with vitamins. He had the luxury of lounging safely indoors whenever he wanted to, but he was not allowed in the bedrooms and never attempted to go there. And he really did seem to be the happiest creature I'd seen.

How much more does God long to give us a good life! He doesn't want to spoil us, but to give us joy, safety, purpose.

How much more, then, will the blood of Christ, who through the eternal Spirit offered himself unblemished to God, cleanse our consciences from acts that lead to death, so that we may serve the living God!

—Hebrews 9:14

Conclusion

The Confidence To Live With
A God Can Do Anything
But Fail Mindset

A minister delivered a sermon in ten minutes one Sunday morning. That was about half the usual length of his sermons. He explained, "I regret to inform you that my dog, who is very fond of eating paper, ate that portion of my sermon which I was unable to deliver this morning."

After the service, a visitor from another church shook hands with the preacher as he was leaving, and said, "Sir, if that dog of yours has any pups, I sure would like to get one to give to my minister."

I know this book has been much longer than a ten minute sermon, and I'm proud of you for sticking with it. This is powerful, life-changing stuff, but that doesn't mean it's easy.

Paul uses a lovely metaphor to encourage Colossians to grow up in Christ: walking with him. Let's end with this encouraging thought.

Walk Confidently

If simple faith is walking with Jesus after receiving Him, imagine what kind of gait we would have. I suppose some might have a picture of trailing a few feet behind the Master with short, fearful steps; after all, we are so unworthy to be in His presence. Some might picture a bored shuffling of feet, like a teenager wishing to be someplace more exciting.

Scripture, however, gives an entirely different picture, one of fullness and power.

> For in Christ all the fullness of the Deity lives in bodily form, and you have been given fullness in Christ, who is the head over every power and authority. In him you were also circumcised, in the putting off of the sinful nature, not with a circumcision done by the hands of men but with the circumcision done by Christ, having been buried with him in baptism and raised with him through your faith in the power of God, who raised him from the dead.
>
> —Colossians 2:9–12

When we accept the grace of God, we become new people; we become heirs of Christ. We are given purpose and boldness. That boldness comes from an awareness of who we are: ambassadors for Christ.

Imagine if you were captured in a jungle by cannibals and brought back to their village. You could talk all you want about how important you are and what a big mistake they are making, but you are nothing to them—other than a nice steak sandwich. How different the situation would be if you could say to the chief, "I came here on behalf of your father who is king on the other side of the jungle; he sent me here to say he loves you and forgives you and wants you to come home." (You might also mention that the king said not to eat you.) Suddenly you would have authority.

Likewise, when we walk in the power of Jesus, we have authority—not based on who we are, but on who

He is. When we humbly accept the Lordship of Christ, we gain confidence. When we walk in our own strength, though, our blessing disappears.

> Blessed is the man who does not walk in the counsel of the wicked or stand in the way of sinners or sit in the seat of mockers. But his delight is in the law of the Lord, and on his law he meditates day and night.
> —Psalm 1:1-2

In light of the power given to us by walking with Him, God's law suddenly takes on new meaning. It's not intimidating or boring—it is empowering and lifegiving.

Walk Alertly

Gary Preston tells the story of a young man who applied for a job as a Morse code operator back when the telegraph was the fastest means of long-distance communication.

> Answering an ad in the newspaper, he went to the address that was listed. When he arrived, he entered a large, noisy office. In the background a telegraph clacked away. A sign on the receptionist's counter instructed job applicants to fill out a form and wait until they were summoned to enter the inner office.
>
> The young man completed his form and sat down with seven other applicants. After a few minutes, the young man stood up, crossed the room to

the door of the inner office, and walked right in. The other applicants perked up, wondering what was going on. Why had this man been so bold? They muttered among themselves that they hadn't heard any summons yet. They took more than a little satisfaction in assuming the young man who went into the office would be reprimanded for his presumption and summarily disqualified for the job.

Within a few minutes the young man emerged from the inner office escorted by the interviewer, who announced to the other applicants, "Gentlemen, thank you very much for coming, but the job has been filled by this young man."

The other applicants began grumbling. Then one spoke up saying, "Wait a minute — I don't understand something. He was the last one to come in, and we never even got a chance to be interviewed. Yet he got the job. That's not fair."

The employer said, "I'm sorry, but all the time you've been sitting here, the telegraph has been ticking out the following message in Morse code: 'If you understand this message, then come right in. The job is yours.' None of you heard it or understood it. This young man did. So the job is his."[47]

How many times have we missed an important word from God, or made a major mistake, or overlooked something or somebody—all because we were not alert to the voice of God. When we walk, we have to be care-

[47]Gary Preston, *Character Forged from Conflict* (Bethany, 1999).

ful to keep our ear tuned to His voice so we will not miss anything He says to us. The way to be familiar with His voice is to be familiar with Him—to spend time with Him daily in prayer and worship.

It's also important to have our hand firmly in His so we won't be led astray. How awful it would be to think we're walking with Jesus only to discover He went one way and we went another. And if we are not alert, not paying attention to what is God's Truth and what is worldly truth, it could happen.

How do you keep your hand in Jesus'? Spend time in the Word, reading and studying scripture so you will know exactly what you believe. Meet with other Christians to help you understand difficult concepts. Pray that the Holy Spirit will enlighten you.

Consider these passages:

See to it that no one takes you captive through hollow and deceptive philosophy, which depends on human tradition and the basic principles of this world rather than on Christ.

—Colossians 2:8

Therefore let us leave the elementary teachings about Christ and go on to maturity, not laying again the foundation of repentance from acts that lead to death, and of faith in God.

—Hebrews 6:1

Walking with Christ is an adventure full of twists and turns that take us to unexpected places. It is no stroll through the park. Well, it is sometimes through green pastures, but at other times He leads us through the valley of the shadow of death. He introduces us to the down and outs of the world, He swoops us past the arrows of our unseen enemies, and He brings us to high places.

Consider the early church, which was far more aware of the dangers of walking with Jesus than we tend to be today:

> The church in Jerusalem endeavored to learn more about the Christian faith and employ the principles of Jesus' teaching. Believers exhibited a remarkable attitude toward life and people, and acknowledged the presence of the supernatural in their everyday adventures. They placed their faith at the center of their life.[48]

Hold tight. Be alert. Enjoy the walk.

Walk Victoriously

It may be a precarious journey walking with Jesus but it's not unsafe. The victory has already been won! Jesus defeated the enemy when He freely gave up His life, and God raised Him from the dead. One day, the Lord will return—and for now, our task is to bring others to Him.

We're not without resources as we do this task. Jesus said to his disciples, "You will receive power when the Holy Spirit comes on you; and you will be my witnesses

---

[48]George Barna, *Revolution*.

in Jerusalem, and in all Judea and Samaria, and to the ends of the earth" (Acts 1:8).

The power of the Holy Spirit? For us? What abundance! We have been given so much!

Remember, though, that when much has been given, much will be demanded (Luke 12:48). We walk victoriously because the battle is won, but there is still much work to be done.

> If any man builds on this foundation using gold, silver, costly stones, wood, hay or straw, his work will be shown for what it is, because the Day will bring it to light. It will be revealed with fire, and the fire will test the quality of each man's work. If what he has built survives, he will receive his reward.
>
> —1 Corinthians 3:12-14

Walk Circumspectly

The danger of walking victoriously is that we forget how the battle was won: through pure and holy love. To remain victorious in our own lives, we must live out that love as we relate with others. As Scripture says, "Make every effort to live in peace with all men and to be holy; without holiness no one will see the Lord" (Hebrews 12:14).

It would be easy to be so caught up in the spiritual thrill of walking with Jesus that we consider the people around us to be unimportant. May it never be! The very reason Jesus came to earth was because the Father loved the people He had made. Far from being unimportant to Him, people are the very thing that matter to him!

As we walk with Jesus, let's look around with love at the others who are walking with him, walking away from Him or walking near him without even knowing who He is. Let's respect and love each other, living in such a way that the One we walk with will be pleased.

Endure hardship with us like a good soldier of Christ Jesus. No one serving as a soldier gets involved in civilian affairs—he wants to please his commanding officer. Similarly, if anyone competes as an athlete, he does not receive the victor's crown unless he competes according to the rules. The hardworking farmer should be the first to receive a share of the crops. Reflect on what I am saying, for the Lord will give you insight into all this. Remember Jesus Christ, raised from the dead, descended from David. This is my gospel.

—2 Timothy 2:3–8